PELICAN BOOKS

THE INVASION OF COMPULSORY SEX-MORALITY

Wilhelm Reich was born in Galicia in 1897. He entered the Medical School of the University of Vienna in 1918, and in 1920, while still a medical student, he was accepted as a member in the Vienna Psychoanalytic Society, then under the direction of Sigmund Freud. His close association with Freud and psychoanalysis continued until 1934. In 1930, Reich left Austria and went to Berlin where he was active in mental-hygiene work and lectured at the Psychoanalytic Clinic and the Marxist Worker's College. Hitler's assumption of power forced him to leave Germany and for the next six years he worked in exile in Denmark, Sweden, and finally Norway. In 1939 he left Europe for the United States where he established a research laboratory in Forest Hills, N.Y. and later in Maine. In 1947 he became the subject of an investigation by the Food and Drug Administration and in 1954 a complaint for an injunction was issued against him. Reich refused to be forced into court as a 'defendant' in matters of basic natural research and the injunction was issued on default. He was subsequently accused of criminal contempt in disobeying this order and sentenced to two years' imprisonment. He died in a federal penitentiary on 3 November 1957.

WILHELM REICH

The Invasion of Compulsory Sex-Morality

PENGUIN BOOKS

Penguin Books Ltd, Harmondsworth, Middlesex, England
Penguin Books Australia Ltd, Ringwood, Victoria, Australia
Penguin Books (N.Z.) Ltd, 182–190 Wairau Road, Auckland 10, New Zealand

—

First English-language publication based on a draft translation
by Werner and Doreen Grossmann of
Der Einbruch der Sexualmoral by Wilhelm Reich

First published in the U.S.A. by Farrar Straus and Giroux, Inc. 1971

First British edition published by Souvenir Press
(Educational and Academic) Ltd 1972
Published in Penguin Books 1975

—

—

Made and printed in Great Britain by
Richard Clay (The Chaucer Press), Ltd,
Bungay, Suffolk
Set in Monotype Garamond

Love, work and knowledge are the well-springs of our life. They should also govern it.

WILHELM REICH

Contents

PART II. THE PROBLEM OF SOCIAL
SEX-ECONOMY

Note

THE first edition of *Der Einbruch der Sexualmoral* was published by the author in 1932. It was followed by a second, enlarged edition in 1935. In 1950, two teachers in Switzerland voluntarily translated this latter edition into English and sent the manuscript to Reich. Anticipating its publication, Reich made extensive corrections and revisions on this draft translation and expanded the title to include the word 'compulsory' and added a new preface which he dated 1951. All of these changes, written by Reich in English, were subsequently translated into German and together with the 1935 German edition serve as the definitive text from which the present edition has been prepared.

New York, 1971   MARY HIGGINS, Trustee
                The Wilhelm Reich Infant Trust Fund

Preface to Third
(First English Language) Edition

THE clinical and ethnologic material for this book was compiled between 1920 and 1930. It was rounded out by the extraordinary material Bronislaw Malinowski presented in 1930 in his comprehensive book *The Sexual Life of Savages*. My study of the origin of human sexual morality was written in September 1931, in the midst of the social storm that rocked the German republic before Hitler's ascendancy to power; and the strong political slant of this book stems from the experiences of that period. Nothing of what shook our social existence at that time (1930–45), in the *political* sense, has survived. However, the facts about the history of human character development have not only survived the last twenty years but have gained in consistency and social influence, which is, in the long run, the true social power.

The sharp discrepancy between the screaming of a cruel political vagrant and the calm efficiency of a study of basic problems of human nature may well serve as a warning today when a differently coloured but basically similar political noise is disturbing our peaceful endeavours to learn and to do ever better in determining the path humanity has been travelling towards new forms of existence over the past few decades. In a few years the big noise will have died out again, and humanity will continue on its journey with less anguish, or so we hope.

Not a single term in sociology, once of such great significance, can today be used without creating confusion. This is due to the *prostitutes in politics*, the '*freedom pedlars*' who have succeeded in destroying every vestige of clear, honest thinking for the sake of mere fact-finding. To them, every term has become a tool of political cheating. In these decades we have begun to turn our attention to an understanding of man's compulsion towards subservience and Führer idolatry. Quite unaware of what they are doing, the Führers misuse the helpless mass individual's sexual and mystical longings for happiness. Accordingly, since the early 1920s *social sex-economy* has devoted itself to a study of this social phenomenon, which is entirely new and has never before been dealt with in sociology. Yet, quite naturally, the new type of mass-psychological thinking grew within the old frameworks of social inquiry and terminology. Nothing can better show the gradual dissolution of the old views and the emergence of the new mass-psychological aspect of social upheaval within the last thirty years than the invalidation of every term pertaining to the old terminology and the affirmation of the new mass-psychological (sex-economic) way of thinking. Thus, most of the terms that have become obsolete during the past twenty years could be eliminated without in the least changing the sex-economic context of this book. The economistic movements, which derive from Karl Marx's influence on sociology, have lost their base of operation with the emergence of a completely new type of human and social problem. Further, the great difficulties these movements have encountered after coming to power, in whatever country, reflect their helplessness in matters human and sexual. The scope of human and social problems is far deeper and broader than Marxian economics encompasses. Time marches on, and political movements remain sitting on one spot. New human strivings emerge and correct the trends in public awareness of social processes.

The problem today is no longer that there is oppression and slavery and the need for liberation from every kind of suppression. This is self-evident to everybody, conservative, liberal, and socialist alike. The problem is how people can take it all and why they irrationally follow the politicians who add to their oppression and who manage totally to exclude the crucial human problems from public debate. *What is going on in people that they follow so much political nonsense* is the problem of the mid-century and it will remain as the major worry in the years to come.

This book was the first step in approaching the answer to this problem. It was followed by *The Mass Psychology of Fascism* (1933) and *The Sexual Revolution* (1929–35). *The Mass Psychology of Fascism* applied the principles of individual and social sex-economy to the new movement of irrationalism among masses of average people. *The Sexual Revolution* investigated the processes in the first half of the twentieth century that were related to sexual and mental mass hygiene. This new social trend has been firmly rooted and is flourishing in the widespread awareness in the United States of the problem of human nature.

These two major works dealing with contemporary social sex-economy could not have remained valid for two decades – as they in fact have, up to and beyond the mid-century – had they not been preceded by a careful study of the history of social sex-economy and mass psychology, beginning in the early twenties. The historical investigation, which was supported by work in clinics with people suffering from the plague of emotional diseases (*Character Analysis*, 1st ed., 1933), introduced several crucial viewpoints into the theory of mental hygiene and the formation of human character structure: *the dynamics and effects of sex-affirmative regulation of human sex-economy*, the first such attempt in the history of science; *the clear distinction between primary, bioenergetically determined, and secondary, culture-made drives*, never drawn before; *the principle of sex-economic self-regulation*, as distinct from the 'idea' of self-regulation without any bioenergetic principle (the *bioenergetic law* of sex-economy provided psychosociology with some natural scientific principles upon which investigations could be based); *clear-cut affirmation and support of infantile and adolescent genitality; the function of the armouring of the character structure in man* as fostered in patriarchal, authoritarian civilizations (cf. *Character Analysis*, 3rd ed., 1949).

These new principles in the theory of human character formation, simultaneously supported by and based on *ethnologic*, *clinical*, and *sociological* material, have begun to turn the tide in the knowledge of human nature – heretofore swamped by lack of scientific principles, mysticism, moralistic prejudice, and educational brutality towards children and adolescents – into the channels of a more rational procedure in biosocial thinking which began to emerge slowly and cautiously in mid-century, particularly in the United States.

Although early orgonomic (sex-economic) pioneer work had broken the trail towards a *life-affirmative, sex-positive attitude* in matters of mental hygiene in the twenties and early thirties of this century, the general stream of works in this field is still paralysed by fear of touching the hot potato I took from the fire of an over-aged, prejudiced moralism in psychiatry and sociology and had to carry alone for two full decades. But the result was worth the strenuous effort. The turn in matters of mental hygiene is here to stay and will develop into great accomplishments. The life-affirmative, non-moralistic, rational trend in biopsychiatry and sociology quietly and determinedly bypasses what is left over from the old, over-aged, prejudiced thinking in matters of 'human nature'.

The discovery of the *Life Energy* (*Orgone Energy*) in the late thirties added further strength to the general efforts finally to get at the *emotional plague* that has ravaged human life and civilization for such a very long time. To have laid some of the basic foundations for this structure in medicine, education, and sociology is in itself a great reward.

Orgonon, Rangeley, Maine, USA   W.R.
July 1951

Preface to Second Edition

THE time that has elapsed since the publication of the first edition has brought two important confirmations of the views presented here: first, the family-political measures of National Socialism in Germany, which completely fit in with the patriarchal ideology of fascism and its way of reproducing itself socially (I have dealt with this in a more recent publication, *The Mass Psychology of Fascism*); second, the results of Roheim's expedition, which place the theory of the invasion of sexual morality into primitive culture on a broader empirical basis than was possible until now – as a matter of fact, they do so without Roheim's intent, even against his own basic theoretical position. This is shown in the Appendix.

As for the rest, the book appears with minor changes only.

November 1934   WILHELM REICH

Preface to First Edition

THE purpose of this investigation into a period of the history of sex-economy is to provide part of the foundation for a systematic social sex-economy. It is necessary to give an introductory survey explaining the development of the approach to the problems dealt with in this book.

Having proceeded from natural science to psychiatry and psychoanalysis, I was very impressed by the possibilities of causal, i.e. theoretically well-founded, psychoanalytic therapy of psychic illnesses. This therapy showed up very favourably against the purely intuitive or, even more so, the superficial persuasion methods of the old school. Although psycho-analytic therapy was far behind the theory of neuroses, a wealth of possibilities for unifying psychological theory and psychotherapeutic practice appeared from a first acquaintance with the subject matter. One knew, after all, that a neurosis had to be understood to be cured, and one could rely on this knowledge, even if very often overwhelmed by failures in everyday practice. The greater the interest aroused by therapeutic problems, the more apparent it became that there was no better avenue of approach to the understanding of the still largely unsolved problems of the origin of neuroses than the consistent pursuit of the question: How can the sick psychic apparatus be made healthy? As we observed the process of transformation of the psychic mechanisms in the course of treatment, we were ever-conscious of the question: What differentiates the psychically healthy individual from the psychically sick? Thus, a deeper insight into the dynamics of the psychic apparatus was made possible.

Freud's original formula – neurosis is a product of an unsuccessful sexual repression; therefore, the first prerequisite for its cure is the elimination of sexual repression and the liberation of the repressed sexual drives – leads to the question:

What happens to the liberated drives? In psychoanalytic literature there were two answers: (1) The sexual desires, having become conscious, can be controlled or condemned. (2) The drives may be sublimated – an important therapeutic way out. The necessity for direct sexual gratification was nowhere mentioned. In the course of many years' experience I have found that the overwhelming majority of sick people do not have the capacity for sublimation necessary for the cure of a psychic illness. The control and condemnation of liberated infantile instinctual drives always proves to be merely a pious hope if the individual's sex life has not been put right; that is, when treatment has not given the patient the capacity for satisfactory and regular sexual intercourse. It quickly became clear that neurosis does not exist without genital disturbances and gross signs of sexual stasis. Psychic illness, through the fixation of infantile sexual attitudes, prevents the development of a normal genital organization and therefore of an ordered sexual economy. Furthermore, the establishment of full genital organization and *genital gratification* proved to be the essential and indispensable factor for a cure. Only genital gratification, as distinct from non-genital sexual drives, is capable of dispelling sexual stasis, thus withdrawing the source of energy from neurotic symptoms. When one had got this far and realized that here was the key to sex-economy and thus to the therapy of neuroses, experience showed that genital organization could be established even in serious cases but that the convalescent's environment thwarted the cure. That happens in the most varied situations. The chastity of an unmarried seventeen- or eighteen-year-old girl from a middle-class home is strictly guarded. In the case of a girl from the lower classes, social conditions (housing problems, contraception problems, the severely moralistic attitude of the parents) are so wretched that the patient, who in treatment tried very hard to shed her neurosis, is forced by the social barriers against sexuality to retreat into neurosis. As a child she had been destroyed by the denial of her sexuality and now she could get well only with great difficulty, if at all, because of the external denial of her genitality. It is very much the same for the unhappily married woman who is economically dependent on her husband or who has to consider her children. It also became clear how difficult it was for a neurotic person who was on the way to recovery to find a suitable partner. The disturbances of potency and the acts of sexual ruthlessness of the men, as well as the sexual disturbances and character deformities of the women, who as sexual partners were to complete the cure, were an additional problem. The very social conditions that in childhood had triggered the neurosis now thwarted the adult's cure, even though in a different form. To this was added the criticism of my colleagues, arising from my contention that no cure of a neurosis was possible without the establishment of a satisfactory genital love life, a criticism that at first seemed rather curious. They opposed my view and insisted that sublimation or the renunciation of sexual happiness was essential. It made me feel more and more strongly that the social barrier was operative here. In view of the clear-cut clinical data, the neglect of these problems in the existing literature must have the same origin: *in the overwhelming majority of cases, the consistent causal therapy of neuroses demanded that the patient should overcome the established social moralism.* One shrank from that. And the repeated checking of the therapeutic formula over a period of years, again and again, produced the same result: neurosis was a product of sexual repression and of the stasis of sexual energy; its cure presupposed the elimination of repression and the establishment of a healthy genital life. Yet everything in social life conflicted with the practical application of this formula.

In addition, there was the difficulty that the vast majority of people in our culture were infected with sexual and neurotic disturbances; and since the only causal therapy, psychoanalysis, required treatment over a long period of time, the problem of the prophylaxis of neuroses naturally arose. There was little point in concentrating on individual therapy. One could only marvel at the fact that the prophylaxis of neuroses had not even been mentioned, or if it had been occasionally, the only answer had been vague phrases. The question, then, was: How are neuroses to be prevented?

Official psychopathology, despite Freud, still clung to the primary importance of hereditary etiology. That this erroneous and fruitless concept has its sociological basis in the need of reactionary research to distract attention from the conditions of the outside world became quite clear later through the study of Marxian sociology.

A straight path led to Marx, once one had recognized that the sexual conditions of man's childhood were the cause of neuroses and later the factors thwarting a cure. The problem resolved itself into several separate questions. Freud had recognized the child's conflict with the parents, especially its sexual component, the Oedipus complex, as the central element in the etiology of neuroses. Why did the family have this function? Neurosis originates in the conflict between sexuality and the denying outside world. Sexual repression comes, then, from society. The family and education as a whole exercise sexual suppression with all the means at their disposal. Why? *What social function have family upbringing and the sexual repression effected by it?*

Freud maintained that sexual repression was the most important prerequisite of cultural development; culture was built on repressed sexuality. For a time one could accept this, but eventually it could not be overlooked that the sexually ill, neurotic person was, culturally, by no means the equal of the sexually healthy, gratified person. The class problem was nowhere near being tackled yet, but the treatment of workers and employees at psychoanalytic clinics brought closer the world of the poorer classes, a sexual and material world strangely in contrast with that which one had come to know in the treatment of private patients who paid well: different sexual views, yet, simultaneously, the same as were found among the middle class. Particularly astonishing was the family upbringing that, sexually and otherwise, ruined all classes alike. Psychoanalysis had criticized this upbringing so little, and when it had, it had done so most insufficiently and mildly. Everyday experience indicated that psychoanalysis was the sharpest instrument for the criticism of sexual upbringing. Why wasn't it used? This upbringing, this destroying of the sexuality of infants, this misery of puberty, genital suppression in marriage – in short, all the social phenomena imposing sexual repression on the individual and creating a mass plague – could not be the prerequisite of cultural development. At psychoanalytic and psychiatric clinics, psychic disturbances were seen on a mass scale. Had we been rendered one-sided by our profession? I began studying my immediate environment and more distant environments as well. Everywhere, with rare exceptions, I found the same deformity of sexual life, the same neurotic plague in the most varied forms, here as an inhibition of the activity of a talented person, there as a marital quarrel, elsewhere as a character deformity; and everywhere there were genital disturbances, symptom and character neuroses, even in people one would never have suspected of being affected. Freud was right in asserting that the whole of mankind was his patient. He had come to understand neuroses clinically, but he had not drawn the obvious conclusions. What, then, was the social reason why man was turned into a neurotic? Had it always been so?

After I had rejected Freud's assertion that sexual repression was an essential part of the cultural development of society, considerable time passed before the realization that sexual repression stems from society evolved into the further question: *What interest has society in sexual repression?* Sociology did not provide any answer except the stereotype statement: 'Culture requires morality.' Finally I came across Marx and Engels, who enabled me to understand much of the mechanism of our material existence, and I was amazed that I had attended secondary school and university without ever having heard of them. Later I understood why.

According to Marx and Engels, class interest and class conflict determine our present-day existence, also our philosophy and our research; behind their objectivity, class interest is operative. Morality is a social product that rises and then passes away, and in the class state it is in the service of the ruling class. Engels's *The Origin of the Family* leads into ethnology. Thus, morality has developed from something else, and the family did not exist at the onset of civilization as has been maintained. Morgan's historical discoveries were very gratifying to me. But his findings and the basic interpretation of the social process by Marx and Engels were at variance with Freud's *Totem and Taboo*. Marx maintained that material conditions of existence determine moral concepts, and this was clearly confirmed by everyday experience. Freud derived morality from a single event, the murder of the primeval father. According to him, this event brought guilt feelings into the world and was the origin of sexual repression. Thus, it is true that he offered a social event as explanation of the origin of sex repression, but he derived this event not from the conditions of existence but merely from man's jealousy towards the primeval father. This proved to be the cardinal point of the whole complex of problems. And it was closely linked with the practical interest in the prophylaxis of neuroses. If Freud was right, if sexual suppression and instinctual restriction were an integral part of the development of civilization and culture, and if further, as was beyond doubt, sexual suppression created neuroses *en masse*, the case for the prophylaxis of neuroses was hopeless. But if Morgan's and Engels's accounts of the history of the family were correct, morality was bound to change again sometime, and, thus, the problem of the prophylaxis of neuroses, and, further, of sexual misery, could be solved. Could, but not necessarily would, for it was not certain that the further transformation of morality would meet the requirements of sex-economy.

To learn about the sociology of sexual disturbances, of perversions, of sexual anti-sociality, one had to investigate the sexual experience of primitive peoples. Sexologic and ethnologic literature provided an over-abundance of reports. It was an established fact that many primitive peoples lived differently, but others were said to hold the same moral concepts as our civilized world, above all with regard to marriage morality. No solution presented itself, for the reports were at variance. They were distorted by moral evaluations or they showed the eagerness of the authors to justify our moral laws, either by attempting to prove that the family and marriage order had always existed, as for instance, Wester-marck tried to show, or by praising our 'progress' from the stage of 'savagery' and 'licentiousness' (Ploss and others). But, simultaneously, there were lyrical reports on the sexual paradise of the primitives, alongside lamentations by scientific and ethical literature over the decline of present-day morality. The first impressions were merely confusing. The only certainty was that the bulk of ethnologic literature was moralistically biased. Primitive peoples, at least many of them, had different conceptions and experienced sexuality differently; and the lower classes also produced their own sexual morality, which differed from that of the middle class.

It was natural, then, to want to learn the facts concerning the revolution in sexual ideology in the workers' and farmers' state of Soviet Russia. The reactionary press was raving about the downfall of culture and morality brought about by the social revolution. But the wording of Soviet sexual legislation was startlingly simple and matter-of-fact. It was totally different from reactionary sexual legislation, and it showed a complete lack of respect for the 'achievements of culture', hitherto so vehemently defended, and for the 'ethical nature' of man. Abortion permitted, even legalized; public assistance in matters of birth control; sexual enlightenment of the young; abolition of the term 'illegitimate'; virtual elimination of compulsive marriage; abolition of punishment for incest; elimination of prostitution; real equality for women, etc. – all these clearly showed that *morality was transformed in a sex-affirmative sense*, reversing completely hitherto existing conditions. But the reactionary press and reactionary scholarship went on raving about the 'decline of culture'. Was Freud right, after all?

A visit to the Soviet Union quickly revealed not only that there was no decline of culture, but strangely enough, the moral atmosphere seemed, at first, ascetic: no sexual importuning in the street; reserve and seriousness everywhere; prostitution still in existence, true, but not seriously affecting the character of the towns; lovers here and there, but not nearly as many as in Vienna or Berlin; at social gatherings an absence of the sexual allusions and smutty conversation characteristic of our circles. In addition, one heard curious anecdotes: If a man dared slap a woman's backside or pinch her cheek, as sometimes happens in our part of the world, he might well be prosecuted before the party tribunal if he was a party member. But the question whether one wanted to become a sexual partner was being asked more and more openly and unhesitatingly: sexual companionship without any underhandedness, women's genitality a matter of course. An acquaintance was in the eighth month of pregnancy, but nobody had asked who the child's father was. A family offered to put up a visitor but didn't have enough room, so the sixteen-year-old daughter said openly to her parents: 'I'll go sleep with X [her boyfriend].' Two members of a youth commune asked to be bound for support of a girl, as both had slept with her and either might be the father of her child. In obstetric clinics, pregnancies were legally aborted. In the Kulturpark, a public establishment and accessible to any adolescent, charts and illustrations on procreation, birth, contraception, and venereal disease were available. At the same time, among the old doctors there was the same shyness about sexual matters as there is among us, for in many instances sexology is still the domain of moralizing and sexpsychologically untrained urologists and physiologists. There were contradictions of course, but there was an overall sex-affirmative change, with a new matter-of-fact attitude towards these problems. The old ways, including clerical marriage morality, persisted only in circles of academics and old civil servants. It was a clear change, not in any way final yet, but showing the economic outlines of a future sex hygiene of the masses in the impressive efforts to raise all members of society to a high cultural level through higher wages and shorter working hours as well as cultural mass education and a stand against religion.[1]

1. [1934] This process has since met with serious obstacles and has partly given way to a regression to attempts at regulation. Soviet sex-economy will be dealt with in a special detailed publication.

[1951] In this interval, the USSR regressed to complete reaction in

Notwithstanding this change in objective sexual existence, there was a noticeable absence of a corresponding sexual theory. Psychoanalysis had declined, owing to its false excursions into sociology and to several reactionary publications by analysts; also, it had completely ignored the major revolutions then in progress. Moreover, in the last few years a clear retreat from the strict and revolutionary libido-theory had been taking place within psychoanalysis. With Freud's first publications on the ego and the death instincts, there was a flood of attempts to desexualize the theory of neuroses and restate it in terms of the theory of the death instinct. Theories were proposed that sought the origin of suffering in a biological 'will to suffer', in the need for punishment and in the death instinct, instead of in the external circumstances of existence. As a psychoanalytic clinician, I could not follow this change. Clinical experience clearly contradicted it, and Marxian sociology made it possible to understand it. Psychoanalysis, originally a revolutionary theory of sex and of the psychology of the unconscious, began to adapt itself, in so far as the theory of sex was concerned, to the authoritarian conditions of existence, thus becoming acceptable to a reactionary society.

It could not be said that in Soviet Russia the revolutionary character of the psychoanalytic theory of sex had been recognized or that it had been rejected because it had turned reactionary, but the latter fact nevertheless made its acknowledgement more difficult. The various Marxist critics of psychoanalysis, in addition to not being sufficiently acquainted with the subject matter, overlooked the change in psychoanalytic theory that turned it from a branch of knowledge that aroused antagonism in reactionaries to one that aroused their enthusiasm. As the opponents of Marxism rejected the sociological excursions of psychoanalysis, and thus its clinical psychology, so the friends of Marxism supported psycho-

sexual matters, in full agreement with its development of a rampant imperialism, imperilling the world under the dogma of 'progress'. This book, together with many other sex-economic writings, has been suppressed in and banned from countries dominated by red fascism.

analytic sociology because clinical psychology made sense to them. Since there is no satisfactory theory of sexuality except the psychoanalytic, which is denied, the change in sexual life in the Soviet Union is taking place far more subconsciously, influenced far less by subjective guidance than is the change in outlook concerning other problems of cultural existence.[2] On the basis of clinical experience, it was evident that the sexual upbringing of children and adolescents would be endangered unless backed by analytically established facts. On the other hand, the sexually freer atmosphere had enabled persons in positions of authority to see many of the facts psychoanalysis had uncovered; for example, the conversion of sexual energy into work interest (sublimation – *'Pereklut-schenie'*). The fact of infantile sexuality was also known here and there; but psychoanalysis was rejected. In the discussion after a lecture at the Neuropsychological Institute in Moscow, a high official of the Board of Public Health said they were waiting for a workable theory of the prophylaxis of neuroses. I was sorry to have to say that none yet existed. But, both from the medical and from the sociological points of view, such a theory must be worked out.

Returning from the Soviet Union with encouraging and stimulating impressions, I got down to the task of ascertaining the present-day political meaning of sexual suppression in reactionary society, through practical work in close touch with the working-class movement. The institution of marriage and family soon emerged as the fixed point around which the struggle in the sexual field revolved, although at that time still subterraneously. It was wrecking sex research and sex reform. An outline of this problem and its solution was given in my book *Geschlechtsreife, Enthaltsamkeit, Ehemoral. Eine Kritik der bürgerlichen Sexual reform.*[3] Perhaps the most important result of my political work for future sex-sociological in-

2. How clearly and systematically religion is being eliminated through the enlightenment of the masses by the natural sciences and the workers' development of technology!

3. Translated into English as 'The Fiasco of Sexual Moralism', Part I of *The Sexual Revolution.*

vestigations was the discovery that sexual suppression is one of the cardinal ideological means by which the ruling class subjugates the working population. *The problem of the sexual misery of the population can only be solved by a movement towards freedom from any kind of oppression. Less pleasant was the thought that the final elimination of the effects of thousands of years of sexual suppression and the establishment of a satisfactory love life for the people, thus eliminating the plague of neuroses, will be possible only when work-democracy has been established and consolidated in the world and the economic security of the population is guaranteed.*

Once the framework for further study had been created, I had to prepare for difficult theoretical work on the foundations of sex-economy. It could never be allowed to lose touch with clinical facts or it would risk bogging down in empty theorizing. Also, I had to reckon with the fact that sexual suppression is rooted in the suppressed masses themselves, and not much was known of the way the different strata of the population would react to having the question brought up, since the core of the problem was undoubtedly marriage and the family and the genital life of children and adolescents. Many years' experience in the sex-political field and particularly in clinics for sexual consultation convinced me that people were waiting for an answer to these problems just as eagerly as they awaited an answer to the problem of their immediate economic existence. At the moment a young but resolute sex-political movement, under revolutionary leadership, is spreading throughout Germany.

The attempt to explain sexual disturbances and neuroses historically nearly failed because the existing ethnologic literature had not considered inner experiences, the character of genital gratification, and the problem of neuroses. One could not rely on such books as R. Schmidt's *Indischen Liebeskunst*, for they gave recommendations but no description of the sex life of foreign peoples. They also failed to consider the relation between sex life and economy. The remaining literature, which attempted a description of this relationship – for instance, the work of Cunow, Müller-Lyer, and others – restricted itself to a discussion of the external forms of marriage and family and did not go into the genital function or actual sexual experience. Only the Morgan–Engels theory was reliable. In view of all this, the investigations of Malinowski attracted my attention because they established the connection between sexual forms and economy in the sex life of matriarchal primitive peoples. Also, they supplied material on actual sexual experience, including the problem of neuroses, which we had long been waiting for. His discoveries exceeded all expectations.

On the basis of this new material, which was a direct continuation of the investigations of Morgan and Engels, one could risk tackling the ethnologic side of the problem of sex-economy. The results are given in this book. I hope that, in the details given here, I have not made any gross ethnologic blunders. If that should nevertheless be the case, I can only ask the reader to consider that I had to work with existing ethnologic literature. The possibility of personal ethnologic research has not been granted, at least until now; I would welcome such an opportunity. However, let me add that, provided my basic historical concept of sex-economy is correct, a few mistakes in details should not be taken too seriously. The study of ethnologic literature has convinced me that even expert knowledge does not shield one from making gross errors in matters concerning sex life.

Berlin, September 1931   WILHELM REICH

PART ONE

THE ORIGIN OF SEXUAL REPRESSION

Sex-Economy in Matriarchal Society

In 1929 a detailed report appeared on the sexual life of the Trobrianders by the anthropologist, Bronislaw Malinowski. He had spent several years on the Trobriand Islands of north-west Melanesia, studying the matriarchal organization of these primitive people.[1] We are indebted to Malinowski for a description, not only the first of its kind but the most thorough, of sexual relationships in connection with economic and social foundations, which we will quote in Chapter 2. Where Malinowski is not expressly quoted, the reader will find analytic results of my own, based on his investigations. They enable us to give ethnologic proof for some of the laws of sex-economy.

The sexual misery in authoritarian, patriarchal society is a result of its intrinsic sexual negation and suppression, which create sexual stasis, which in turn begets neuroses, perversions, and sexual crime. For that reason a society that has no interest in sexual suppression must be free from sexual misery. Historically speaking, so long as, and to the extent that, there is no such interest, it will remain free from sexual misery. We can then say that the members of such a society live *sex-economically*, by which we only mean that they have a *naturally regulated energy economy*.

We then must inquire how sexual life is regulated, and we anticipate that it is by means of *the gratification of the sex instinct* and not by moral standards. We are prepared to find in the sex life of the Trobrianders almost exactly the opposite of

1. *The Sexual Life of Savages in North-Western Melanesia.* Quotations and page numbers refer to the Harcourt, Brace & World edition. Also quoted in this book are Malinowski's *Sex and Repression in Savage Society* (1927) and *Crime and Custom in Savage Society* (1926). Page numbers for these books refer to the editions published by Routledge & Kegan Paul, London. Used by permission.

what is found in the sex life of the members of our society: undisturbed sex life of children and adolescents and full capacity for gratification in the genitally mature – i.e. orgastic potency of the mass individual.

THE SEX LIFE OF CHILDREN
AMONG THE TROBRIANDERS

Let us begin with childhood and examine what Malinowski says. The natives have their first sexual experiences at a very early age. 'The unregulated and, as it were, capricious intercourse of these early years becomes systematized in adolescence into more or less stable intrigues, which, later on, develop into permanent liaisons' (p. 51).

The child's freedom and independence extend also to sexual matters. To begin with, children hear of and witness much in the sexual life of their elders. Within the house, where the parents have no possibility of finding privacy, a child has opportunities of acquiring practical information concerning the sexual act. I was told that no special precautions are taken to prevent children from witnessing their parents' sexual enjoyment. The child would merely be scolded and told to cover its head with a mat. (p. 54)

This admonition has nothing at all to do with sex-negation. It is merely a measure to prevent those having coitus from being disturbed. The children can examine each other and otherwise play sexually as much as they like. It must be emphasized that in spite of, or rather because of, sexual liberty in childhood, voyeurism as a perversion does not occur. From this, all those who are afraid of its implications can learn – if psychoanalytic investigation into the origin of perversions has not already convinced them – that freedom for the partial sex instinct in childhood does not of itself lead to perversions unless there are conditions of otherwise suppressed sex life. Further:

There are plenty of opportunities for both boys and girls to receive instruction in erotic matters from their companions. The children initiate each other into the mysteries of sexual life in a directly practical manner at a very early age. A premature amorous existence begins among them long before they are able really to carry out the act of sex. They indulge in plays and pastimes in which they satisfy their curiosity concerning the appearance and function of the organs of generation, and incidentally receive, it would seem, a certain amount of positive pleasure. Genital manipulation and such minor perversions as oral stimulation of the organs are typical forms of this amusement. Small boys and girls are said to be frequently initiated by their somewhat older companions, who allow them to witness their own amorous dalliance. As they are untrammelled by the authority of their elders and unrestrained by any moral code, except that of specific tribal taboo, there is nothing but their degree of curiosity, of ripeness, and of 'temperament' or sensuality, to determine how much or how little they shall indulge in sexual pastimes.

The attitude of the grown-ups and even of the parents toward such infantile indulgence is either that of complete indifference or of complacency – they find it natural, and do not see why they should scold or interfere. Usually they show a kind of tolerant and amused interest, and discuss the love affairs of their children with easy jocularity. I often heard some such benevolent gossip as this: 'So-and-so (a little girl) had already had intercourse with So-and-so (a little boy).' And if such were the case, it would be added that it was her first experience. An exchange of lovers, or some small love drama in the little world would be half-seriously, half-jokingly discussed. The infantile sexual act, or its substitute, is regarded as an innocent amusement. 'It is their play to *kayta* (to have intercourse). They give each other a coconut, a small piece of betel-nut, a few beads or some fruits from the bush, and then they go and hide, and *kayta*.' But it is not considered proper for the children to carry on their affairs in the house. It has always to be done in the bush. (pp. 55–6)

All sorts of [dancing] games, which are played by the children of both sexes on the central place of the village, have a more or less strongly marked flavor of sex. (p. 57)

The fact that Trobriand children play sexually is not the vital point for our study. The great majority of children in our cultural spheres do too, especially those of the lower classes (with the exception of those who are already seriously inhibited neurotically). But, just as in the case of the sexual embrace, the decisive factor is not that it is done but with what inner attitude and in what social surroundings. It is important, then, what attitude educators and parents take towards children, towards their sexual play and their natural motility, generally. It is this, after all, that determines the sex-economic value of these sexual activities. We stress the point because this view is not given any space in sexologic literature, which merely registers the fact that such play occurs, or overlooks it altogether. It was the examination of the economy of the genital function that taught us to consider the act itself less important than the conscious and unconscious psychic attitudes that accompany it.[2] From the beginning of a child's life it has a positive attitude towards sexuality, through the pleasure mechanism. The social surroundings alone determine whether this originally positive attitude can survive or whether it must give way to guilt feelings and genital anxiety, brought to sex life by society in various ways.

Now it has been shown that among the Trobrianders the parents' attitude not only is not disturbing but is rather benevolent and friendly. We can say, therefore, that, with the exception of the incest taboo, there is *no sex-negating morality*. On the contrary, a clearly *affirmative* ego develops and, as we shall see later, a *sex-affirmative ego ideal*.[3] As sexuality is free,

2. See my interpretation of orgastic potency in *The Function of the Orgasm*.

3. [1934] However slight the difference may appear to be between mere toleration and the affirmation of infantile and pubertal sex life, it is decisive for the psychic structure formation of the child. The tolerant attitude of educators that is found today in certain small circles must be looked upon as complete sex-negation. Not only does the child experience the toleration as the non-punishment of something actually prohibited, but the mere toleration or 'permission' of sexual play does not constitute a counterweight to the overwhelming pressure of the social atmosphere. The explicit and unmistakable affirmation of infantile love life on the part of educators, however, can become the basis of sex-affirmative elements of the ego structure, even when it cannot palliate the social influences. This view is intended as a criticism of the attitude of those psychoanalysts who dare not take the important step from toleration to affirmation. Replying that this has to be left to the children is nothing but a shifting of responsibility. If, in the analysis of children, adolescents, or

the incest taboo cannot be considered a sexual restriction, since abundant possibilities for gratification of a sex-economic nature remain. One cannot speak of restriction of gratification of the food instinct if the eating of mutton and green peas is banned but the person can eat as much of any other vegetable or meat as he pleases. We stress this in opposition to the many assertions that instinctual life among primitive peoples is restricted. These restrictions have no economic-dynamic importance. An economically and dynamically excessive incest wish is found where there is too great an interest in the incestuous object because of a *general* restriction of instinctual life. This is true of all other excessive instinctual impulses and explains the fact that the primitive is quite conscious of the incest *prohibition* but it need not be repressed because the incest wish does not particularly stand out from other desires as long as the other desires are gratified.

Every Trobriand boy knows that he must not look upon his sister as a sexual being. The conscious avoidance of any intimate contact shows the consciousness of sexual feelings towards the sister. If sexual life were otherwise forbidden, the incest desire would, because of the local and familiar contact with the sister, immediately increase to such an extent that a profound repression of the desire would become necessary. This desire would then have to seek an unhealthy outlet. These facts are essential for the understanding of the *intensity* of the incest wish among our own children. Apart from the natural ties to parents and brothers and sisters, it is to a large extent the result of the complete denial of other sexual relationships; and not least among the causes are the sexual ties of the parents to the children, which in turn are conditioned by the sex starvation of the adults.

---

adults, no counterweight to social influences is offered, the removal of sexual repression remains theoretical. Just as wrong as it would be to force on a person something not organically desired, is it necessary to support in the child or in sick people such tendencies as work in the direction of sex-economy. Between the toleration of sexuality and its affirmation, the social sexual barrier is operative. Affirming sexuality means stepping beyond the sexual barrier.

It is typical of the Trobriand upbringing that in other respects too the parents' attitude towards the children lacks any of the authoritarian features inherent in our educational measures. We come to a full understanding of the intimate relationship of sexual denial and sexual suppression, on the one hand, and other characteristics of patriarchal upbringing, on the other, when we hear their opposite among the Trobrianders, described as follows:

Children in the Trobriand Islands enjoy considerable freedom and independence. They soon become emancipated from a parental tutelage which has never been very strict. Some of them obey their parents willingly, but this is entirely a matter of the personal character of both parties: there is no idea of a regular discipline, no system of domestic coercion. Often as I sat among them, observing some family incident or listening to a quarrel between parent and child, I would hear a youngster told to do this or that, and generally the thing, whatever it was, would be asked as a favour, though sometimes the request might be backed up by a threat of violence. The parents would either coax or scold or ask as from one equal to another. *A simple command, implying the expectation of natural obedience, is never heard from parent to child in the Trobriands.*

People will sometimes grow angry with their children and beat them in an outburst of rage; but I have quite as often seen a child rush furiously at his parent and strike him. This attack might be angrily returned; but the idea of definite retribution, or of coercive punishment, is not only foreign, but distinctly repugnant to the native. Several times, when I suggested, after some flagrant infantile misdeed, that it would mend matters for the future if the child were beaten or otherwise punished in cold blood, the idea appeared *unnatural* and *immoral* to my friends, and was *rejected with some resentment*.

Such freedom gives scope for the *formation of the children's own little community*, an independent group, into which they drop naturally from the age of four or five and continue till puberty. As the mood prompts them, they remain with their parents during the day, or else join their playmates for a time in their small republic. And this community within a community acts very much as its own members determine, standing often in a *sort of collective opposition* to its elders. If the children make up their minds to do a certain thing, to go for a day's expedition, for instance, the grown-ups and even the chief himself, as I often observed, will not be able to stop them. In my ethnographic work I was able and was indeed forced to collect my information about children and their concerns directly from them. Their *spiritual ownership in games and childish activities was acknowledged*, and they were also quite capable of instructing me and explaining the intricacies of their play or enterprise. (pp. 52–3; Reich's italics)

Under dictatorial régimes the authoritarian suppression of the child serves to produce an expediently submissive structure in conformity with the organization of society in general, which constantly reproduces itself in the child. Just as here the parents are the executive instruments of the ruling order, and the family its ideological factory, similarly, matriarchal society, in so far as it is still distinct, reproduces itself ideologically by allowing the psychic structure of the child to develop freely. In this way the social ideologies of this society are fully developed in the children's community. And, just as in authoritarian society sexual suppression becomes the basis for psychic inhibitions, in matriarchal society sexual freedom becomes the basis of characterological freedom, thereby guaranteeing libidinously well-founded social ties between the members of the society. These facts prove that self-regulation of the sexual life of the community is possible through instinctual gratification (in contrast to moral regulation).

THE SEX LIFE OF ADOLESCENTS

Let us now turn to the sex life of Trobriand adolescents. We see sexual conflicts, it is true, and a certain amount of psychic suffering springing from the difficulties of many love relationships, but we note the absence of external restriction. We see no 'pubertal neuroses', no suicides, no asceticism 'for culture's sake'.

As the boy or girl enters upon adolescence the nature of his or her sexual activity becomes more serious. It ceases to be mere child's play and assumes a prominent place among life's interests. What was before an unstable relation culminating in an exchange of erotic manipulation or an immature sexual act becomes now an absorbing passion, and a matter for serious endeavour. An adolescent gets definitely attached to a given person, wishes to possess her, works purposefully towards this goal, plans to reach the fulfilment of his desires by magical and other means, and finally rejoices in achievement. I have seen young people of this age grow positively miserable through ill-success in love. This stage, in fact, differs from the one before in that personal preference has now come into play and with it a tendency towards a greater permanence in intrigue. The boy *develops a desire to retain the fidelity and exclusive affection* of the loved one, at least for a time. But this tendency is not associated *so far with any idea of settling down to one exclusive relationship*, nor do adolescents yet begin to think of marriage. A boy or girl *wishes to pass through many more experiences*; he or she still enjoys the prospect of complete freedom and has no desire to accept obligations. Though pleased to imagine that his partner is faithful, the youthful lover does not feel obliged to reciprocate this fidelity . . .

This group lead a happy, free, Arcadian existence, devoted to amusement and the pursuit of pleasure . . .

Many of the taboos are not yet quite binding on them, the burden of magic has not yet fallen on their shoulders . . .

. . . Young people of this age, besides conducting their love affairs more seriously and intensely, widen and give a greater variety to the setting of their amours. Both sexes arrange picnics and excursions and thus their indulgence in intercourse becomes associated with an enjoyment of novel experiences and fine scenery. They also form sexual connections outside the village community to which they belong. Whenever there occurs in some other locality one of the ceremonial occasions on which custom permits of licence, thither they repair, usually in bands either of boys or of girls, since on such occasions opportunity of indulgence offers for one sex alone. (pp. 63–5; Reich's italics)

Psychoanalytic ethnologists have tried to derive from the puberty rites of many primitive organizations the thesis that among these, too, pubertal activities are punished, just as they are with us, with the one difference that the punishment precedes the person's entrance into genital love life. But a study of ethnologic literature makes one suspicious of interpretations that all too clearly show a tendency to justify our circumstances ethnologically and lightly apply to other social organizations interpretations that apply only to phenomena originating in our own circumstances. In saying this, it is not my wish to question the truth of these theories. When we are able to determine the economic interests which influence and transform sexual life, then the theories will be important to us. If one considers sex-economy historically, it seems quite improbable that punishments for adolescent genitality have their roots in the instinctual structure of man (ambivalence, hatred, jealousy, etc.). There are organizations, as for instance the Trobrianders', in which not only is there no sign of punishment but on the contrary there is outright public support (the *bukumatula*, the adolescent consecrations and festivals, etc.). The representatives and supporters of the punitive view, which is so one-sidedly biopsychological, would first have to explain why in this organization the desire for sexual power and other negating qualities are absent. We maintain that these punitive attitudes towards pubertal sexuality are a result of the influence of economic interests on purely natural genital gratification, and we are about to prove this.

Let us return to our subject. The sex-affirmation goes as far as social assistance:

To meet this need, tribal custom and etiquette offer accommodation and privacy in the form of the *bukumatula*, the bachelors' and unmarried girls' house of which mention has already been made. In this a limited number of couples, some two, three, or four, live for longer or shorter periods together in a temporary community. It also and incidentally offers shelter for younger couples if they want amorous privacy for an hour or two ... At present there are five bachelors' establishments in Omarakana, and four in the adjoining village of Kasana'i. Their number has greatly diminished, owing to missionary influence. Indeed, for fear of being singled out, admonished and preached at, the owners of some *bukumatula* now erect them in the outer ring, where they are less conspicuous. Some ten years ago my informants could count as many as fifteen bachelors' homes in both villages, and my oldest acquaintances remember the time when there were some thirty. This dwindling in number is due, of course, partly to the enormous decrease of population, and only partly to the fact that nowadays some bachelors live with their parents, some in widowers' houses, and some in the missionary compounds. But whatever the reason, it is needless to say that this state of affairs does not enhance true sex morality ... I was told that sometimes a man would build a house as a *bukumatula* for his daughter, and that in olden days there used to be unmarried people's houses owned and tenanted by girls. I never met, however, any actual instance of such an arrangement. (pp. 70–72)

The *ulatile* (adolescent) has either a couch of his own in a bachelors' house, or the use of a hut belonging to one of his unmarried relatives. In a certain type of yam-house, too, there is an empty closed-in space in which boys sometimes arrange little 'cosy-corners', affording room for two. In these, they make a bed of dry leaves and mats, and thus obtain a comfortable *garçonnière*, where they can meet and spend a happy hour or two with their loves. Such arrangements are, of course, necessary now that amorous intercourse has become a passion instead of a game.

But a couple will not yet regularly cohabit in a bachelors' house (*bukumatula*), living together and sharing the same bed night after night. Both boy and girl prefer to adopt more furtive and less conventionally binding methods, to avoid lapsing into a permanent relationship which might put unnecessary restraint upon their liberty by becoming generally known. That is why they usually prefer a small nest in the *sokwaypa* (covered yam-house), or the temporary hospitality of a bachelors' house. (p. 66)

This social assistance in providing a place for the embrace is the best expression of a social sex-affirmation, going far beyond mere toleration. Similarly, the indifference to and active hindering of adolescents in authoritarian society, which manifests itself in its failure to provide a place for the embrace, is in harmony with its sex-negative attitude. Whereas social assistance has a decisive positive influence on the sexual health of adolescents among the primitives, its hindrance in authoritarian society results in a crippling and debasing of love life. It does not prevent the embrace from taking place. But the embrace is carried out in haste and anxiety in corridors and corners of fences and hedges, instead of in tranquillity in hygienic places.

And what about 'culture', to which the timid continuously refer? The brothel life of our own youth should be compared with the following facts:

To call this institution 'Group Concubinage' would lead to misunderstanding; for it must be remembered that we have to deal with a number of couples who sleep in a common house, each in an exclusive liaison, and not with a group of people all living promiscuously together; there is never an exchange of partners, nor any poaching nor 'complaisance'. In fact, a special code of honor is observed within the *bukumatula*, which makes an inmate much more careful to respect sexual rights within the house than outside it. The word *kaylasi*, indicating sexual trespass, would be used of one who offended against this code; and I was told that 'a man should not do it, because it is very bad, like adultery with a friend's wife.' (p. 73)

Within the *bukumatula* a strict decorum obtains. The inmates never indulge in orgiastic pastimes, and it is considered bad form to watch another couple during their love-making. I was told by my young friends that the rule is either to wait till all the others are asleep, or else for all the pairs of a house to undertake to pay no attention to the rest. I could find no trace of any 'voyeur' interest taken by the average boy, nor any tendency to exhibitionism. Indeed, when I was discussing the positions and technique of the sexual act, the statement was volunteered that there are specially unobtrusive ways of doing it 'so as not to wake up the other people in the *bukumatula*.' (p. 73)

The adolescent couple are not tied to each other by any law or custom; they are kept together by personal attachment and sexual passion and can separate at will. We understand that this relationship does not include any right of possession. Either partner is free to embrace other partners, especially on the occasion of the harvest and moon festivals. Expressions of jealousy do occur, but on certain occasions even this is immoral, as for example when after a death the young girls comfort the mourning men with sexual embrace. In spite of all this – or, from the point of view of sex-economy, precisely because of it – the relationships (without external or internal compulsion) are frequently more lasting, more intimate, and more satisfying than those achieved by our sexually crippled youth.

The common interests of the couple are purely sexual. For instance, they never have their meals together. We shall learn later that common meals are the symbol of marriage.

We see how inadequate the bombastically learned categories of 'monogamy', 'polygamy', 'promiscuity', are to describe these sexual relationships, which are directed and regulated solely by the satisfaction of *genital* needs. These couples are monogamous, occasionally polygamous, and at festivals even promiscuous; but these classifications themselves have no meaning in this society and only come to mean something and have importance as moral evaluations in a society such as ours which tries to subject life to moralistic regulation. With us, too, they do not correspond to the facts. Our sexual relationships are also highly varied. The difference between us and primitive peoples – this must be stressed, as it separates our sex-economic views from all others in every respect – does not lie in the fact that they live polygamously or promiscuously and we monogamously; nor can a claim for monogamy be postulated from the monogamous lives of primitive peoples, as many sexologists and ethnologists have tried to maintain. It depends exclusively on the manner in which sex life is regulated by society and in the *different way of experiencing* the embrace that results. The genital apparatus itself has the same nature everywhere, notwithstanding race differences and the phylogenetic influence of thousands of years of sex suppression (weakening of the somatic sexual apparatus?). And what causes our sexologists to rack their brains is that the genital apparatus does not know their categories, their '-gamies', but only the goal of instinctual gratification. The question, then, is whether the particular social order is willing to recognize this function, and whether or not it can do so. That, however, is a sociological problem.

As adolescents grow older, their relationships become more firm and enduring – which, as we have shown elsewhere,[4] must be ascribed to the gradual satiation of the sensual needs after puberty. This, in turn, causes tender attachments to arise. If there were no institution of marriage, these relationships would not last forever either but would give way to others in the course of time. However, under prevailing circumstances, the firmer relationships turn into marriage. First,

4. See Part I of *The Sexual Revolution*.

though, there is a probationary period during which the young couple test their attachment and constancy and the parents take necessary steps, i.e. make economic preparations. *At this point, sexual needs encounter specific economic interests.*

SEXUAL FESTIVITIES

The advanced sexual culture of the Trobrianders finds expression primarily in various celebrations having no goal but sexual play and subsequent gratification. These differ from similar celebrations of youth in our society, first in that their real purpose is not hidden; second in that there is no denial of, inner resistance to, or outer inhibition of final gratification; and third in the absence of genital anxiety and guilt feelings, such as corrode the genital gratification of our adolescents if they allow themselves the final gratification. 'He has not to stumble upon the final fulfilment of erotic desire, he immediately anticipates it. All the customs, arrangements, and codes of behaviour dictate simple, direct approach' (p. 311).

Another essential difference is the absence of any kind of sentimentality in sexual relationships; yet the sex life of the Trobrianders is not devoid of a certain romanticism. This shows up the nature of the sexual sentimentality artificially nurtured by reactionary fiction and exploited by publishers: it presupposes the inhibition of final gratification, being itself an inadequate substitute for it, and it means there is continuous orgastic longing that is never fulfilled.

Thus there is nothing roundabout in a Trobriand wooing; nor do they seek full personal relation, with sexual possession only as a consequence. Simply and directly a meeting is asked for with the avowed intention of sexual gratification. If the invitation is accepted, the satisfaction of the boy's desire eliminates the romantic frame of mind, the craving for the unattainable and mysterious. If he is rejected, there is not much room for personal tragedy, for he is accustomed from childhood to have his sexual impulses thwarted by some girls, and he knows that another intrigue cures this type of ill surely and swiftly. (pp. 313–14)

Thus, we see that where genitality is fully developed there is no tendency to prolong unhappiness through unrequited love, and we are better able to understand this tendency, which is typical of our youth. It is the result of an overestimation of the sexual object caused by the prevention of final gratification. Our revered experts in the problems of adolescence ascertain 'statistically' that sexual sentimentality and bad verse are 'intrinsic to puberty'. True! Intrinsic to puberty among *our* adolescents, who grow up under conditions that sap their vitality.

With the Trobrianders and other primitive peoples, in so far as they have not fallen prey to emerging patriarchy or to white missionaries, things are different: 'The facts described [above] have shown us that, subject to certain restrictions, everyone has a great deal of freedom and many opportunities for sexual experience. Not only need no one live with impulses unsatisfied, but there is also a wide range of choice and opportunity' (p. 236).

The woman's place in sexual life is no different from the man's: 'In matters of love the Trobriand woman does not consider herself man's inferior, nor does she lag behind him in initiative and self-assertion. The *ulatile* have their counterpart in the *katuyausi*, amorous expeditions of village girls to other communities' (p. 269).

We shall deal with the *ulatile* later, in a different context. Here let us merely give the account of the *katuyausi*:

The *katuyausi* party remained seated, nonchalant and detached . . . The youths and older men stand facing them, pursuing their own conversations with apparent unconcern. Then banter and jokes begin to pass from one side to the other; boys come nearer the girls and the ceremony of choice begins. According to custom, the initiative in pairing off should come from the hosts, and each guest has to accept any offer made to her as a matter of etiquette. But, of course, definite preferences between the outstanding individuals of each group exist and are known. An unimportant boy would not dare interfere with the pleasure of his stronger, older, and more influential comrade, so that in reality the choice is largely based on anterior intrigues and attachments. Each boy then ceremonially offers a small gift to the girl of his choice – a comb, a necklet, a nose stick, a bunch of betel-nut. If she accepts the gift she accepts the boy for that night as her lover. When the boy knows the girl well he presents the gift himself. If he does not, or if he feels too shy, he will ask help of an older man, who hands over the offering with the words, *kam va'otu* (*va'otu* – visiting present, present of inducement), 'So-and-so gives it to you; you are his sweetheart.' Very rarely does a girl refuse or ignore such a present; if she did, she would greatly offend and mortify the man.

After the boys and girls have thus been allotted in pairs, they all, as a rule, go to some spot in the jungle, where they spend the best part of the night chewing, smoking, and singing, each couple keeping to themselves. At times a boy and a girl will leave the main group without any attention being paid to them. Some of the boys may invite their sweethearts to spend the rest of the night in a *bukumatula* of the village, but usually this presents difficulties. All the arrangements associated with the *katuyausi*, as well as with the *ulatile*, are distinguished by complete decorum, and by the absence of all orgiastic elements. They are carried out, no doubt, in a less delicate manner in the southern villages than in the north, but even in the south they essentially differ from such orgiastic customs as the *kamali*, the *bi'u*, and the custom of the *yausa*. (pp. 270–72)

In addition to the *ulatile* of the young men and the *katuyausi* of the young women there is – not actually in the tribe Malinowski studied, but in the more southern and northern communities – the custom of the so-called *kayasa*, during which

the relaxation of all control is complete ... Sexual acts would be carried out in public on the central place; married people would participate in the orgy, man or wife behaving without restraint, even though within hail of each other. This licence would be carried so far that copulation would take place within sight of the *luleta* (sister, man speaking; brother, woman speaking): the person with regard to whom the strictest sexual taboos are always observed ... The trustworthiness of these statements is confirmed by the fact that I was told several times, when discussing other forms of *kayasa* in the north, that all of them were carried out in a much more orgiastic manner in the south. Thus at a tug-of-war *kayasa* in the south, men and women would be on opposite sides. The winning side would ceremonially deride the vanquished with the typical

ululating scream (*katugogova*), and then assail their prostrate
opponents, and the sexual act would be carried out in public. On
one occasion when I discussed this matter with a mixed crowd from
the north and the south, both sides categorically confirmed the
correctness of this statement. (pp. 258–9)

Why this custom has been lost among the Trobrianders we
cannot tell from what Malinowski says. Is it a step in the
development of property interests in the early stages of
patriarchy, or are there other historical reasons? We do not
know. We are told that not very long ago, when the only
strangers who came to the Trobriand Islands were the
members of so-called Tula expeditions (trade between the
islands), the custom was for the girls from the village to visit
the strangers on the beach after the bartering was over. It
was considered a right, sanctified by custom, that the girls
from the village sleep with the strangers; and the girls' lovers
could not reproach them or show jealousy. However this
custom may be interpreted – as a relic of raping incursions of
old by other tribes, or as a primeval form of exogamous love
relationships – the important point for our purposes is that
the ordered life of the community was undisturbed, despite
the absence of sexual moralism.

THE ORGASTIC POTENCY OF THE PRIMITIVES

When we read of institutions such as the *ulatile* and *katuyausi*
expeditions, we feel touched by something strange that is not
in harmony with culture and civilization but, rather, excludes
them. And our cultural fellow beings develop an odd curiosity
to learn about such institutions: a longing for the primeval
paradisiac state emerges. It can easily be shown, however,
that in fact we are longing not for the *ulatile* expeditions but
for the primitive's *capacity for genital experience*. There are
enough *ulatile* and *katuyausi* expeditions among us. Communal visits of students to brothels; youth hikes that lead to
genital activity; masked balls and masquerades, peasant dances
and 'Fensterln',[5] do not differ in principle from the sexual

5. *Fensterln:* climbing in and out of a girl's window (peasant dialect).

celebrations of the primitive except in *one* point, but that point is decisive. Our sexual celebrations end with a hangover because of the unfulfilled expectation of genital gratification, an expectation that is usually hidden from oneself, concealed behind hypocrisy and 'respectability'. These primitive institutions have continued into our time, though in different form, but they have lost their sex-economic value: instead of gratifying, they merely heighten sexual tension. We also retain the initiation of adolescents, but the original meaning is completely veiled and turned into its opposite: instead of an initiation into genital love life, an initiation of intensified church influence for its suppression.

Certainly the genital embrace is no less frequent in our cultural world than in more primitive areas; promiscuity among our young males is in fact more pronounced. Unfaithfulness in marriage is more widespread among us than among 'savages', because of intense moral pressure and disturbances of genitality. On the one hand, moral hypocrisy seeks to persuade us that we are distinguished from the 'savages' by morality, on which we have a monopoly; on the other hand, the breakdown of morality among us is denounced by everyone, from the Pope down to the fledgling Nazi and the reactionary sexologist. Yet the facts are quite plain: *primitive people have a full capacity for the genital embrace; 'civilized' man cannot achieve genital gratification because his sexual structure has been neurotically corroded by the moral inhibitions acquired in upbringing.* Statistical samplings taken at random indicate that, on the average, 90 per cent of women and about 60 per cent of men are psychically ill, sexually disturbed, and incapable of genital gratification. Having reached this conclusion about the basic mechanism of the disordered sexual economy of the members of our society, we must now prove that the sexual function of the primitive is undisturbed and that for him orgastic gratification in the embrace is the rule.

Malinowski, to his great credit, has given us information about the sex life of primitives that is not available anywhere else in the literature, which records only the external forms of the sex act. On the basis of his report, we can therefore present the following proofs for the fact that Trobriand men *and* Trobriand women are orgastically potent:

First, the Trobrianders are convinced 'that white men do not know how to carry out intercourse effectively' (p. 338), that a white man is not capable of making a woman reach orgasm. 'Indeed, to the native idea, the white man achieves orgasm far too quickly' (p. 338). Here we have clear confirmation that the Trobriander knows exactly what the *right* sort of gratification is, and that compared with the morally uninhibited primitive, the white man reaches orgasm too soon. (I have elsewhere designated this as 'physiological ejaculatio praecox', which is typical of men affected by sexual suppressions.) That we are not dealing with racial differences is borne out by the fact that this chronic premature ejaculation, which is not regarded as an illness, can be cleared up by the removal of the acquired sexual inhibitions. The premature ejaculation that occurs among the great majority of men in our culture also involves a considerable reduction of genital gratification, for full gratification presupposes a prolonged friction for the concentration of the whole of the free libido at the genital apparatus.[6]

Evidence of the orgastic potency of the Trobriand women is the fact that the Trobrianders use the same expression for female and male orgasm: both are called *ipipisi momona*, which means 'the seminal fluid discharges ... The word *momona* signifies both the male and female discharge' (p. 339). Besides, it is a matter of course that the man waits for the woman to reach gratification.

From the personal reports of these primitive people, too, their capacity for sexual experience is absolutely clear. Here is what one of them says:

'When I sleep with Dabugera I embrace her, I hug her with my whole body, I rub noses with her. We suck each other's lower lip, so that we are stirred to passion. We suck each other's tongues, we bite each other's noses, we bite each other's chins, we bite cheeks and caress the armpit and the groin. Then she will say; "o my lover,

6. *The Function of the Orgasm.*

it itches very much . . . push on again, my whole body melts with pleasure . . . do it vigorously, be quick, so that the fluids may discharge . . . tread on again, my body feels so pleasant." ' (p. 341)

The reader is asked to compare this knowledge on the part of the primitive with the theories of many of our sexologists, that gratification is not necessarily part of the nature of women, or that nature has arranged things so that women are insensitive in the vagina, and thus do not feel pain when giving birth[7] – and other similar 'scientific' effusions of moralistically prejudiced brains.

The majority of our women are incapable of carrying out the particular rhythmical pelvic movements in the embrace that lead up to their own orgasm and heighten the gratification of the man, an action practised by prostitutes in a conscious and cold manner, to make the man at least think that he is being stimulated. To facilitate this movement, the primitive carries out the embrace in a squatting position and makes fun of the coitus position of the European, which hinders the woman in her counter-movements.

The natives regard the squatting position as more advantageous, both because the man is freer to move than when kneeling, and because the woman is less hampered in her responsive movements . . . Many a white informant has spoken to me about perhaps the only word in the native language which he ever learned, *kubilabala* ('move on horizontally'), repeated to him with some intensity during the sexual act. (pp. 338–9)

The reports of missionaries and prejudiced ethnologists are of little use in the critical evaluation of the genitality of the women of primitive peoples. Unlike Malinowski, they do not derive their knowledge from the natives themselves. For example, the complaints of white men that the native women are difficult to stimulate. Among us, one does not conclude from the sexual frigidity of women that the men are impotent but that 'by nature woman is sexually indifferent or sexually unexacting'; and from such reports by white men

7. Cf. reference to Krische, p. 185.

with a warped genitality, the 'ethnologic proof' can easily be derived.

An adequate sexual education is necessary for the development of orgastic potency. Among the Trobrianders, as has been said, the body and the psychic apparatus are trained from a very early age in the natural technique of producing pleasure in the embrace, which saves them having to learn an artificial 'love' technique later. There are other primitive peoples among whom the teaching of the sex act by women plays a significant role. An important subject for research would be whether this active instruction by adults is not in itself a *reaction to a damaging of the sexual structure* of these primitive people by the patriarchal suppression of infantile sexuality; whether it does not signify a helping hand in the first stages of patriarchy, which is interested in chaste girls but not in the genital disturbance of women.

This is what Angus says about the ceremony of *chensanwali* among the people of Azimba Land, Central Africa, as quoted in Havelock Ellis's *Sex in Relation to Society*:

At the first sign of menstruation the mother takes the young girl to a grass hut outside the village. There, women teach her the facts about sexual intercourse and the different positions in which it is carried out. The vagina is enlarged by means of a horn which is inserted and secured in place by means of bands of bark cloth. When all signs of menstruation have passed the women perform a dance in front of the girl. She is placed on the ground in a sitting position, while the dancers form a ring around her. No men are allowed to be present. The girl is made to go through the mimic performance of sexual intercourse. Through song she is taught about the relation between men and women and about all her duties when she becomes a wife. She is also instructed that during the time of her menstruation she is unclean, and that during her monthly period she must close her vulva with a pad of fibre used for the purpose. She is taught to be *faithful to her husband* and to try to bear children, and she is also taught the various arts and methods of making herself seductive and pleasing to her husband, and of thus retaining him in her power. The whole matter is looked upon as a matter of course and not as a thing to be ashamed of. *The women of this tribe are mostly chaste.*

Further:

In Abyssinia, as well as on the Zanzibar coast, young girls are educated in buttock movements which increase their charm in coitus. To be ignorant of this so-called Duk-Duk is a great disgrace to a girl. Among the Swahili, too, a system of hip movements is cultivated. From sixty to eighty young women practice this buttock dance together for some eight hours a day, laying aside all clothing, and singing the while. The public are not admitted . . . At the end of three months the training is over, and the girl goes home in festive attire. Similar customs are said to prevail in the Dutch East Indies and elsewhere.

This report certainly contains exaggerations, but we need have no doubt about the existence of sex instruction. The fact that these women live chastely, or in strict marital faithfulness, points to advanced patriarchy, and our supposition that here we are dealing with attempts to eliminate the disturbed genitality of the women becomes more probable.

NO NEUROSES – NO PERVERSIONS

If the greater part of a society lives sex-economically, there can be no neuroses, simply because these disorders arise from inhibited genital life. That is the conclusion we must reach if we follow consistently the libido theory and the theory of neuroses.[8]

A further result of our sociological investigations into the origin and effect of sex-negating morality is the discovery that it is this morality that brings about sexual repression and gives rise to sexual stasis. In so doing, it turns everyday psychic conflicts into neurotic ones. Further, we conclude from the psychoanalytic investigation of perversions that, ultimately,

8. [1934] I alone bear the responsibility for this view. Freud and his school reject it and oppose it; they do not want to see it upheld in the name of psychoanalysis. I have to agree with Freud on that point: this fundamental view of sex-economy arose when the orgastic function of genitality was discovered and introduced into psychoanalytic theory. It has basically changed our understanding of the economy of psychic ill-nesses, however. This is what has caused the gap between sex-economic theory and the present-day psychoanalytic theory of neuroses.

they are the consequence of the deflection of sexual energy from its normal genital goal. Through this inhibition of genitality, all pregenital demands are overcharged with energy, so that under certain conditions they emerge as perversions. The fixation on an infantile instinctual goal, which is regarded by psychoanalytic theory as the basis of perversions, is itself the result of the *hindering of the natural genital love life* of children and adolescents by the sex-negating sexual order whose executive agents are the parents.

Since moralistic sex education first enters the history of mankind with the interest in economic gain and develops along with it, neuroses are a feature of a society that has a patriarchal organization. Malinowski's observations and comparative investigations provide irrefutable proof of these connections, while they also convince us of the possibility of self-regulation of sex life by genital gratification.

Besides the still predominantly matriarchal society of the Trobriands which has been described, Malinowski had the opportunity to observe a society of primitive people on the Amphlett Islands, south of the Trobriand Islands. These people, Malinowski wrote, are very similar to the Trobrianders in race, custom, and language but differ from them considerably in social organization. They have a strict sexual morality with regard to the premarital genital embrace, which they condemn, and they have no institutions such as the Trobrianders have to further genital love life. It is significant that their family life is considerably more restricted. Although still organized along matriarchal lines, they have a much stronger patriarchal authority, and 'this, combined with the sexual repressiveness, establishes a picture of childhood more similar to our own' (Malinowski: *Sex and Repression in Savage Society*). Malinowski writes: 'In the Trobriands though I knew scores of natives intimately and had a nodding acquaintance with many more, I could not name a single man or woman who was hysterical or even neurasthenic. Nervous tics, compulsory actions or obsessive ideas were not to be found.' From time to time one comes across cretinism, idiocy, and speech impediments, and also occasional fits of anger and violence. All this is attributed by the natives to black magic. The Trobrianders think, however, that in the Amphlett Islands there is a different kind of 'black magic', which gives rise to various forms of compulsive actions, compulsive thoughts, and nervous symptoms:

... during my few months' stay in the Amphletts, my first and strongest impression was that this was a community of neurasthenics ... Coming from the open, gay, hearty and accessible Trobrianders, it was astonishing to find oneself among a community of people distrustful of the newcomer, impatient in work, arrogant in their claims, though easily cowed and extremely nervous when tackled more energetically. The women ran away as I landed in the villages and kept in hiding the whole of my stay ... I at once found a number of people affected with nervousness.

Even more interesting and significant for our theory of the relation between social organization, sex-economy, and neuroses is what Malinowski says about the Mailu, a community inhabiting the southern coast of New Guinea, who are already completely organized as a patriarchy: 'They have a pronounced paternal authority in the family, and a fairly strict code of repressive sexual morals. Among these natives, I had noted a number of people whom I had classed as neurasthenics, and therefore useless as ethnographic informants' (p. 89). And further:

It is fully confirmed in the Trobriands that free sex life does not allow any homosexuality to form there. It cropped up in the Trobriands only with the influence of white man, more especially of white man's morality. The boys and girls on a Mission Station, penned in separate and strictly isolated houses ... had to help themselves out as best they could, since that which every Trobriander looks upon as his due and right was denied to them. According to very careful inquiries made on non-missionary as well as missionary natives, homosexuality is the rule among those upon whom white man's morality has been forced in such an irrational and unscientific manner. (p. 90)

Here, the economic expansion of capitalist economy is already at work, sending missionaries as a vanguard to prepare the natives with moralism, alcohol, religion, and other 'cultural blessings', in defence and justification of which the emotional plague knows how to avail itself of the best and most gifted researchers. However, we also must say that, of itself, the development of matriarchal society leads necessarily though incomparably more slowly and more gently, to the same type of sexual morality. The missionaries and other white robbers merely accelerate this process and imbue it with the cruelty of the impotent and avaricious 'bearers of culture'.

Let us add what Malinowski reports regarding perversions in his publications on the sex life of the Trobrianders: that there is no 'unnatural sexual activity'. Such manifestations as sodomy, homosexuality, fetishism, exhibitionism, and masturbation are to the natives only miserable substitutes for the natural genital embrace and therefore bad and worthy only of a fool. The idea that he could be incapable of satisfying his drives pleasurably in a natural way would be particularly offensive to a Trobriander's pride. He despises perversions as he despises one who eats inferior or impure things instead of good clean food.

The following are typical remarks on the subject of perversions: 'No man or woman in our village does it.' 'No one likes to penetrate excrement.' 'No one likes a dog better than a woman.' 'Only a *tonagowa* (idiot) could do it.' 'Only a *tonagowa* masturbates. It is a great shame; we know then that no woman wants to copulate with him; a man who does it, we know, cannot get hold of a woman.' In all native statements the unsatisfactory nature of a substitute or makeshift is emphasized, and the implication is of poverty as well as of mental and sexual deficiency. The natives would also quote instances such as that of Orato'u, the village clown of Omarakana, deformed and defective in speech; the several albinos and a few specially ugly women; and say that such people, but not an ordinary man or woman, might practice one perversion or another ... If inversion be defined as a relationship in which detumescence is regularly achieved by contact with a body of the same sex, then the male friendships in the Trobriands are not homosexual, nor is inversion extensively practiced in the islands. For, as we know, the practice is really felt to be bad and unclean because it is associated with excreta, for which the natives feel a genuine disgust. And while the ordinary caresses of affection are approved as between members of the same sex, any erotic caresses, scratching, nibbling at eyelashes, or labial contact would be regarded as revolting. (Malinowski, *The Sexual Life of Savages*, pp. 470, 471)

The Trobriander thus develops a genital pride and a corresponding sense of honour (*sex-affirming ego ideal*) which are an excellent aid to him in evaluating the true nature of perversion. Our sex-negating social atmosphere has managed to keep the best of our sexologists from recognizing this simple connection between the disturbance of potency through the social suppression of natural love life, and perversions as substitute gratifications of genitality. 'In some respects his moral regulations are biologically sounder than our own, in some more refined and subtle, in some a more efficient safeguard for marriage and the family' (p. 440).

Only the first two statements are correct; the genital life of these primitive people is naturally, sex-economically regulated; on this basis, a high sexual culture develops. As to the alleged protection of marriage and the family that this is supposed to entail, however, Malinowski, who in spite of his own investigations has not freed himself from the biological interpretation of the family, gives it as fact.

Such forms of licence as we find in the Trobriands fit so well into the scheme of individual marriage, the family, the clan, and the social group – and they fulfill certain functions so adequately that there remains nothing serious or incomprehensible to explain away by reference to some hypothetical earlier stage. They exist to-day because they work well side by side with marriage and family; nay, for the benefit of marriage and family; and there is no need to assume any other causes for their past than those which maintain them at present. (pp. 537–8)

We shall show, by means of Malinowski's own reports, that the 'unrestrained', biologically regulated genital life of the Trobrianders is, nevertheless, at odds with their institutions of marriage and family. And if we have to take a stand for the 'unrestrained', with no neuroses and perversions, or for marriage and family, with perversions and neuroses and sexual misery, there is nothing left for us but to decide in favour of one or the other.

Whether these complementary perversions of sadism and masochism play a large part in the sexual life of the natives I am unable to say. The cruel forms of caress – scratching, biting, spitting – to which a man has to submit to a greater extent even than the woman, show that, as elements in eroticism, they are not absent from native love-making. On the other hand, flagellation as an erotic practice is entirely unknown; and the idea that cruelty, actively given or passively accepted, could lead, of itself alone, to pleasant detumescence is incomprehensible, nay ludicrous, to the natives. I should say, therefore, that these perversions do not exist in a crystallized form.

Fellatio . . . is probably practiced in the intimacy of lovemaking . . . Receiving my information exclusively from men, I was told that no male would touch the female genitals in this manner, but, at the same time, I was assured that *penilinctus* was extensively practiced. I do not feel convinced, however, of the truth of this masculine version. The expression, *ikanumwasi kalu momona*, 'lapping up the sexual discharges', designates both forms of fellatio. (p. 475)

Masturbation . . . is a recognized practice often referred to in jokes. The natives maintain, however, that it would be only by an idiot (*tonagowa*) or one of the unfortunate albinos, or one defective in speech; in other words, only by those who cannot obtain favours from women. The practice is therefore regarded as undignified and unworthy of a man, but in a rather amused and entirely indulgent manner. Exactly the same attitude is adopted towards female masturbation.

. . . Exhibitionism is regarded by the natives with genuine contempt and disgust.

. . . In the treatment of these deviations of the sexual impulse, it is impossible to draw a rigid line between the use of certain practices – as fellatio, passionate and exuberant caresses, interest in the genitals – when they are used as preliminary and preparatory sexual approaches on the one hand, and as definite perversions on the other. The best criterion is whether they function as a part of courting, leading up to normal copulation, or whether they are sufficient by themselves for the production of detumescence. It is well to remember in this context that the nervous excitability of the natives is much less than ours, and their sexual imagination is relatively very sluggish; that excitation and tumescence are usually achieved only by the direct visual, olfactory, or tactual stimulus of the sexual organs; and that orgasm, in man or woman, requires more bodily contact, erotic preliminaries, and, above all, direct friction of the mucous membranes for its production. It is, therefore, plausible to assume that preparatory erotic approaches with the natives would have less tendency to pass into autonomous acts, that is to develop into perversions, than is the case among nervously more excitable races [pp. 475–6] ... Scenes of frequent occurrence in any public park in Europe, after dark or even before, would never be seen in a Trobriand village [pp. 478–9] ... The whole attitude of the Trobriander towards sexual excess displays an appreciation of restraint and dignity, and an admiration for success; not only for what it gives to a man, but because it means that he is above any need for active aggression. The moral command not to violate, solicit, or touch is founded on a strong conviction that it is shameful; and shameful because real worth lies in being coveted, in conquering by charm, by beauty and by magic. (p. 491)

We see that the moral standards of the Trobrianders are fundamentally different from ours. Among us these standards are derived from general sex-negation; the Trobriander derives them from a *positive* attitude towards genital sex life and feels very clearly the morbid and defective character of perversions. 'When a woman has no men who come to her, and takes the initiative and goes herself to a man, we call her a wanton.' Malinowski, rightly, adds: 'It is clear that the moral censure incurred by such women is founded on the shame that attaches to erotic unsuccess' (p. 489). That applies in our society too, of course, but this evaluation is submerged, it has no official standing. The authoritarian view of discipline and moralism sets a negative mark on such behaviour, not because lack of success is considered a disgrace but because sexual desire outside marriage, and in certain strata of society, within marriage, is so considered. The consequences of these two different standards, the sex-economic and the moralistic, are not minor: the former promotes the full development of genital effectiveness, physical beauty, and attraction; the latter causes the opposite, the crippling of genitality, the hiding and deforming of the body (cf. the church as the enemy of female gymnastics).

Let us look at another example of the Trobriander's sex-economic evaluations. He condemns sexual lasciviousness and lewdness, the typical products of sex suppression. 'Inability to master desire, leading to insistent and aggressive sexuality,' reports Malinowski, 'is regarded with contempt both in man and woman' (p. 488). Here we probably have an inaccuracy of expression. We are certain that the Trobriander disapproves not of the inability to control oneself but rather of the disturbed capacity for gratification which is the pathological basis of sexual aggression. That is clear from the whole attitude of the Trobriander, who, as we know, can have intercourse every day and does not know any genital inhibitions.

At this point we must record an important fact: the neurotic or pervert who previously was lascivious, sexually aggressive, or insatiable because his capacity for gratification was disturbed, after treatment begins to show, in so far as his genitality has been freed from moralistic pressure and he has progressed from sex-negation to sex-affirmation, characteristics similar to those of the Trobriander, who is organized sex-economically from the start – characteristics such as natural modesty, choice of partner on a sex-economic basis, refusal to have intercourse with prostitutes or to engage in masturbation or independent perverse acts. We can say therefore that the removal of moral inhibition allows the sex-economic self-regulation of love life to develop, whereas sexual moralism produces the exact opposite of what is intended.

In the following section we shall deal with the changes in the direction of European and American morality that the development of patriarchy thrusts like a wedge into this sex-economically regulated society. We shall see that with the advance of sexual moralism, and keeping pace with it, the characteristic features of our culture take clear shape, especially as regards the institution of marriage and its economic basis.

2

Economic and Sexual Contradictions among the Trobrianders

MATRIARCHAL ORGANIZATION AND THE RISE OF PATRIARCHY

THE matriarchal organization of the Trobrianders of northwest Melanesia, studied by Malinowski, is particularly well suited to illuminate the obscure history of the origin of sex-negating morality and its connection with the beginning of class division.

Malinowski emphasizes the fact in several places in his report that among the Trobrianders very strange contradictions appear between the matrilineal laws of inheritance and clan division and the part the male, either as mother's brother or as husband, plays in this society. Let us first set forth the material from which we shall later draw our conclusions. At this point we merely anticipate that it will be a question of contradictions between still matriarchal and already beginning patriarchal organization. First, here is what Malinowski has to say about the economic and social organization of the Trobrianders, which, he repeatedly points out, and quite rightly, is the basis for sexual conditions.[9]

The Trobriand archipelago lies to the northeast of New Guinea and consists of a group of flat coral islands that hem in an extensive lagoon. The land is very fertile and the lagoons are rich in fish. The inhabitants of the separate islands trade with each other, just as the people living along the coast trade with those living in the interior of the islands. The economy is based on agriculture and fishing. There is a lively bartering of garden produce for fish and vice versa. Production is communal, and so is distribution. Several times Malinowski

9. The following description is taken from *Crime and Custom in Savage Society*, pp. 9–39.

speaks of ownership practices, and as an example he mentions the canoe. His description of conditions governing the ownership of canoes shows that the economy of the Trobrianders is of a co-operative character. For each canoe there is one rightful owner. The men who constitute the crew of the canoe belong, as a rule, to a sub-clan; they are tied by certain obligations. Whenever the whole community goes out fishing, the owner cannot refuse his canoe. We see that, for them, ownership has little to do with our exclusive ownership of the means of production; that, on the contrary, property is communal. If the 'owner' cannot go out in the canoe himself, he must relinquish the canoe or send someone in his stead. Each man in a group of canoes has a specific place and a specific task and must do his part. Every man, too, receives his fair share of the catch. Malinowski does not mention anywhere that 'ownership' of a canoe entails special privileges. The term *toli* (owner) indicates rank only and merely confers a distinction 'even when it does not give a claim to rights of exclusive use' (*Sexual Life*, p. 24). 'Thus the ownership and use of the canoe consist of a series of definite obligations and duties uniting a group of people into a working team' (*Crime and Custom*, p. 18).

Both the owner and the other members of a group may give up their rights to a relative or friend. This often happens, but always in return for compensation. Malinowski decidedly objects to the interpretation of these conditions as communist and says a modern joint-stock company might be called communist with as much justification. He reports that a definite system of division of functions and of mutual obligations prevails, based on a binding sense of responsibility and on the recognition of the need for co-operation, along with self-interest and privileges. What Malinowski has to say about canoe ownership fits in with Marxist descriptions of primeval communism. The master of the canoe, who is also the leader of the group, must finance the construction of a new canoe (there is a natural economy) when the old one can no longer be used, and he has to maintain it in good condition, with the help of the other members of the canoe group.

Thus the group is always in a state of reciprocal obligation. Each man is entitled to a specific place and the privileges associated with it. In return, he must perform his appointed task and he receives a certain title ('master', 'watcher for fish', 'keeper of the nets', etc.). In other words, joint ownership, division of labour, communal work, and the distribution of products according to the work performed: *primeval communism.*

Two villages usually barter with each other. Part of the catch of fish is retained; the rest is exchanged for the surplus garden produce of another village. Every fisherman is strictly bound to settle his debt to his opposite who sells produce, if he has accepted garden produce from him, and vice versa. Neither partner can refuse; neither can defer it.

The whole legal system, Malinowski writes, is based on the 'symmetry of all social transactions' (*Crime and Custom*, p. 25), on the reciprocity of services. The exchange, then, engenders a system of sociological ties of an economic nature, and the principle of reciprocity replaces the social sanctions of law. Two parties, exchanging services and functions, watch closely the degree of fulfilment and the fairness of conduct of each other. This well-assessed give-and-take creates a free-and-easy atmosphere in which to carry out transactions.

At this point we must break off our description of the economic background. We shall discuss the economic and social structure in detail when we turn specifically to the marriage gift.

The most important factor in the legal system of the Trobrianders is the concept that the mother alone forms the child's body and that the man in no way contributes to its formation. The child, they say, is of the same substance as the mother, but it has no bodily connection whatever with the father; the man's part in procreation is unknown.[10] Consequently, clan division and incest taboos exist along the mother's

10. It is evident that among the Trobrianders the pleasure function is the only basis for genital contact. Contrast this with the attitude of the church, which views genitality as being only in the service of procreation. [*Editor*]

line only. The blood relations on the mother's side constitute a clan; and these clans are divided into sub-clans, which are distinguished by near or remote blood relationship.

The sub-clans are at least as important as the clans, for the members of the same sub-clan regard themselves as real kindred, claim the same rank, and form the local unit in Trobriand society. Each local community is composed of people belonging to one sub-clan, and to one sub-clan only, who have joint rights to the village site, to the surrounding garden-lands, and to a number of local privileges. Large villages are compounded of several minor local units, but each unit has its own compact site within the village and owns a large contiguous area of garden-land. (*Sexual Life of Savages*, p. 495)

Among the members of the sub-clan a strict incest taboo exists. For the clan as a whole the taboo is somewhat milder. The members of a sub-clan consider themselves real blood relations; members of other sub-clans in the same clan are regarded as blood relations in a superficial largely figurative sense. Altogether there are four clans, distinguished according to different totemistic factors. The natives believe that membership in a clan is innate, as bodily characteristics are.

The relationship of the mother's brother to the children is quite different from that of their actual father. The mother's brother is the real head of the family in a matriarchal society. He is the 'guardian' of his sister's children; he teaches them magic rites and the ideals of the clan when they reach adulthood; he is respected by them and is an example to the adolescents who will later inherit from him. At the same time, he has to look after his sister and he is the one who provides the marriage tribute. The husband is an esteemed friend, who lovingly cares for his friend's children as an adult companion and playmate. Obviously, then, children do not develop the attitude towards their fathers that our children do (the term *father*, with reference to the Trobrianders, must be thought of in a purely social sense). Trobriander children regard their father as a friend, not as an authority. Authority devolves on the maternal uncle.

This purely matriarchal principle is found side by side with another, which, at least in its social features, already deserves to be called patriarchal. First of all, marriage is patrilocal – i.e. the wife follows her husband to his village. Only the son of the chief marries 'matrilocally', for which, as we shall see later, there is a special economic reason. Outright property interests of men already prevail, just as the actual power to exercise authority rests with the man, although it derives from the mother's line. Here the original matriarchy comes into conflict with incipient patriarchy. Malinowski, it is true, mentions institutions that give their due to tribal law and its matriarchal claims, as well as to 'the promptings of paternal love, which incline the father to bestow all possible privileges on his son' (p. 95), but it is clear that this 'fatherly love', with its rights and claims, is really economic patriarchy in its first stages. Also, the village community has a chief, and several village communities have a common superior chief, who enjoys many privileges. 'As woman is debarred from the exercise of power, land ownership, and many other public privileges, it follows that she has no place at tribal gatherings and no voice in such public deliberations as are held in connection with gardening, fishing, hunting, oversea expeditions, war, ceremonial trade, festivities and dances' (p. 36).

Here we see such plain signs of patriarchy that we cannot agree with Malinowski that they are only 'promptings of paternal love'. That we are dealing with advancing patriarchal rule can be clearly derived economically from the custom of the marriage tribute. But first let us have a closer look at the chief's position.

It is a very remarkable fact in the constitution of the tribe of which we are speaking, that the source of power is principally economic, and that the chief is able to carry out many of his executive functions and to claim certain of his privileges only because he is the wealthiest man in the community. A chief is entitled to receive tokens of high respect, to command observance and require services; he can ensure the participation of his subjects in war, in any expedition and in any festival; but he needs to pay heavily for all these things. He has to give great feasts and finance all enterprises by feeding the participants and rewarding the chief actors. Power in the Trobriands is essentially plutocratic. And a no less remarkable and unexpected feature of this system of government is that, although the chief needs a large revenue, there is nothing of the sort directly attached to his office: no substantial tributes are paid him by the inhabitants as from subject to chief. The small annual offerings or tribute in special dainties – the first fish caught, vegetable primitiae, special nuts and fruit – are by no means a source of revenue; in fact the chief has to repay them at full value. For his real income he has to rely entirely on his annual marriage contribution. This, however, in his case, is very large, for he has many wives, and each of them is far more richly dowered than if she had married a commoner. (pp. 130–31)

Only the chief is entitled to practise polygamy. Now, ethnologic research has two main schools of thought, opposed to each other. One considers matriarchal organization the original form of human society, from which, in the course of economic development, patriarchy and polygamy evolved. The main supporters of this concept are Morgan and Engels. The other school takes the view that the present-day organization of the family – i.e. the patriarchal one – evolved in primeval times as an original organization in the form of the polygamous primeval horde under the leadership of a strong male. Freud was of this opinion. We do not wish to go into the pros and cons of these two schools and mention them only because among the Trobrianders we find both forms of organization. We must add, however, that those who believe matriarchy was the original form of organization stress the socioeconomic motivating force, whereas the supporters of the patriarchy theory emphasize more the biological-psychological responsibility in the development of human society and the family.

From Malinowski's investigations it can be clearly demonstrated how the transition in social, economic, and ideological conditions from *mother-right* to *father-right* takes place among the Trobrianders. We have here an opportunity to observe a process that we would otherwise have to deduce by logic and through comparisons of wholly matriarchal and patriarchal organizations.

Before we trace this process, let us see what the transition consists of:

1. The transition of power from woman to man. Thereby the power displacement grows vertically, according to rank. The chief, in contrast to the citizen, has the most power; his wives have the least.

2. The transition from natural genital love life to the compulsory marriage bond.

3. The transition from sex-affirmation to sex-negation, from the affirmation of premarital genital activity to a demand for premarital asceticism. And finally the most important thing:

4. The growing division of society into oppressing upper groups and oppressed lower groups.

Thus, we see only the process of transition of power, not its onset. But we are able to observe from the very first stages the beginning of sex-negation and the division into classes. The central mechanism of this process of transition is the ritual of the marriage tribute.

THE MARRIAGE GIFT AS THE DESTROYER
OF MATRIARCHAL SOCIETY

The Wedding

The wedding itself is quite unceremonious. When a permanent relationship has reached a certain maturity, the frequent appearance of the partners together in public is sufficient to express their intention to marry. Divorce is not complicated either. Each partner is entitled to leave the other if he does not wish to maintain the relationship. Here we are dealing with the loose 'pairing marriage' which was first described by Morgan and which is a preliminary stage to our lasting monogamous marriage. But we shall see that the man has a much greater interest in the wedding and the continuance of the marriage than has the woman.

The formalities of divorce are as simple as those by which marriage is contracted. The woman leaves her husband's house with all her personal belongings, and moves to her mother's hut, or to that of her nearest maternal kinswoman. There she remains, awaiting the course of events, and in the meantime enjoying full sexual freedom. Her husband, as likely as not, will try to get her back. He will send certain friends with 'peace offerings' (*koluvi*, or *lula*) for the wife and for those with whom she is staying. Sometimes the gifts are rejected at first, and then ambassadors are sent again and again. If the woman accepts them, she has to return to her husband, divorce is ended and marriage resumed. If she means business, and is determined not to go back to her wedded life, the presents are never accepted; then the husband has to adjust himself as best he may, which means that he begins to look for another girl. The dissolution of marriage entails in no case the restitution of any of the inaugural marriage gifts exchanged. (p. 146)

As long as the marriage lasts, the marriage bond ties the couple 'firmly and exclusively'. This bond is upheld by law, morality, and custom.

In marriage, for the first time, we come across moralistic demands and manifestations, as well as the typical results of compulsory marital morality, which do not seem so strange to us as does the Trobrianders' premarital life: the bonds are firmer, faithfulness demanded, unfaithfulness punished. Jealousy and adultery now disturb love life most strongly. 'Any such breach of marital fidelity is as severely condemned in the Trobriands as it is in Christian principle and European law; indeed the most puritanical public opinion among ourselves is not more strict' (p. 115). Does that not sound as though compulsory morality were inborn in man? We shall not allow ourselves to be thus led astray. Comparing this practice with the customs of the Catholic Church and American puritanism, we shall conclude, rather, that there are qualitatively similar reasons for each of them.

To begin with, some characteristic features of the emerging sex-negation should be noted. No reference whatsoever to the sexual relations of the couple or to their former love life is allowed, and an infringement of this custom is considered indecent. The first period after their wedding is marked by abstinence.

Although there is no definite sexual taboo at this time, the newly wedded couple probably think less of love-making during the stage which corresponds to our honeymoon than they have done for a long time previously. I have heard this statement volunteered: 'We feel ashamed in the house of our mother and father. In the *bukumatula* a man has intercourse with his sweetheart before they marry. Afterwards they sleep on the same bunk in the parental house, but they do not take off their garments.' The young couple suffer from the embarrassment of new conditions. The earlier nights of marriage are a natural period of abstinence. (p. 110)

Whereas, previously, taking meals together was an impossible, even indecent act, now these common meals become the very symbol of married life by which the intention to marry, or the fact that marriage has taken place, is proclaimed. Strict regulations as to decency come into force. The couple must not display any gesture that might betray a tender relationship between them. The married woman may not have secret love affairs, which are exactly what give the youth the best opportunity for sexual relations. It is as though custom itself knew that what is added to love life through compulsory marriage not only has nothing to do with genitality but on the contrary is at odds with it.

There is an interesting and, indeed, startling contrast between the free and easy manner which normally obtains between husband and wife, and their rigid propriety in matters of sex, their restraint of any gesture which might suggest the tender relation between them. When they walk, they never take hands or put their arms about each other in the way, called *kaypapa*, which is permitted to lovers and to friends of the same sex. Walking with a married couple one day, I suggested to the man that he might support his wife, who had a sore foot and was limping badly. Both smiled and looked on the ground in great embarrassment, evidently abashed by my improper suggestion. Ordinarily a married couple walk one behind the other in single file. On public and festival occasions they usually separate, the wife joining a group of other women, the husband going with the men. You will never surprise an exchange of tender looks, loving smiles, or amorous banter between a husband and wife in the Trobriands. (pp. 111-12)

When the pair move on to their own hut, they may or may not share the same bunk; there seems to be no rule in this matter. Some of my native authorities specifically informed me that married couples always sleep in the same bed at first, but later on they separate and come together only for intercourse. I suspect, however, that this is rather a piece of cynical philosophy than a statement of accepted usage. (pp. 110-11)

Interestingly enough, with marriage cynical considerations arise. Further:

It must be remembered that it is impossible to get direct information from any man concerning his own conjugal life; for in this matter a very strict etiquette has to be observed. In speaking to a husband the slightest allusion to this must be avoided. Nor is any reference allowed to their common sexual past, nor to the woman's previous love adventures with other men. It would be an unpardonable breach of etiquette were you to mention, even unwittingly and in passing, the good looks of a wife to her husband: the man would walk away and not come near you for a long time. The Trobriander's grossest and most unpardonable form of swearing or insult is *Kwoy um kwava* (copulate with thy wife). It leads to murder, sorcery, or suicide. (p. 111)

Here we see a code of conduct come into play that strikes one as *forced avoidance*. Consider the contradiction between the free genital life before marriage and the hampered genitality in marriage. This allows no interpretation but that certain interests intervene here to restrict sexual freedom in marriage, mobilizing psychic attitudes in their support that are similar to psychic defence (repression). Malinowski endeavours in his work to present marriage as generally harmonious. Yet there are tragic accounts of wives' suicides and of marital conflict, and there is the 'veil' that falls over the Trobriand marriage situation. These betray the beginnings of all the contradictions common among us – i.e. between the sexual interests, which aim towards a relationship of limited duration, and the social ones, which aim towards indissolubility.

Until marriage, sexual life was completely free and satisfied;

with marriage, severe inhibitions of genitality occur and great obligations are assumed. Malinowski enumerates several reasons for marriage:

1. The Trobriander enters into his full social status only when he is married.

2. Custom imposes the moral obligation of marriage.

3. 'There is, further, the natural inclination of a man past his first youth to have a house and a household of his own' (p. 81); the services the wife renders the husband are tempting.

4. 'The woman, who has no economic inducement to marry, and who gains less in comfort and social status than the man, is mainly influenced by personal affection and the desire to have children in wedlock' (p. 82).

Here we are given a number of moral and biological reasons for marrying, but none of them accounts for the existence of the institution of marriage itself. Rather, the reasons given reflect psychic interests and moral attitudes engendered by the social institution of marriage itself – interests and attitudes by which this institution is rooted in the character structure of the individual. Full social status could be recognized without marriage; the custom itself requires a sociological explanation. The woman could satisfy her personal inclinations without marriage, since, apart from marriage, there is the lasting sexual relationship. And finally, the concern to have children born in wedlock derives from the concern for the institution of marriage. Therefore, unlike Malinowski, we believe that the economic interest of the man cannot be regarded as one among several other interests, but that the decisive role, not only in the marriage contract but in the establishment and preservation of the institution, must be ascribed to him, for:

Another very important reason for marriage, from the man's point of view, is economic advantage. Marriage brings with it a considerable yearly tribute in staple food, given to the husband by the wife's family. This obligation is perhaps the most important factor in the whole social mechanism of Trobriand society. On it, through the institution of rank and through his privilege of polygamy, rests the authority of the chief, and his power to finance all ceremonial enterprises and festivities. Thus a man, especially if

he be of rank and importance, is compelled to marry, for, apart
from the fact that his economic position is strengthened by the
income received from his wife's family, he only obtains his full
social status by entering the group of *tovavaygile*. (p. 81)

Let us consider further the 'most important factor in the
whole social mechanism of Trobriand society.' It will provide
an answer to quite a few riddles of this society and also to the
problem of the origin of compulsory sexual morality and the
division into classes.

The 'Only Lawful Marriage'

Through marriage the husband acquires economic claims on
his male relations by marriage, who 'in exchange for their
services, retain a legal authority over the wife and her children'
(p. 129). In view of the process set in motion by the ritual of
the marriage gift, we should say 'retain for some time'. Let
us look at all the facts.

Until her marriage, the girl's family did not take any
interest in her sexual relationships. She was allowed to do as
she pleased. The marriage, however, for the girl's family is
'a matter of constant and considerable effort and worry',
and is eagerly discussed by her relatives, but they are barred
from exerting any influence on the marriage plans. All
interest is focused on the marriage gift.

The custom of the marriage gift is very complicated. Gift
and countergift, which to begin with are exchanged by the
parents of the marriage candidates, *give way to a yearly tribute
from the relatives, especially from the wife's brothers to the husband
and his family after the wedding, which has to be paid regularly and
for the duration of the marriage.* The countergifts, which are now
given by the husband's family to his wife's, are acts of cour-
tesy; they are by no means equivalent to the marriage gifts
from the wife's family. The marriage gift consists mainly of
garden produce. The size of the tribute varies according to the
rank of the persons concerned, but in an average household it
amounts to about half the year's consumption. Everyone keeps

part of his garden produce for himself; the rest goes to the female relatives and their husbands. But the marriage gift – as Malinowski emphasizes – 'is the chief and most ostentatious product of the garden work' (p. 124). Ideologically, the marriage tribute represents what is 'the chief pride of a Trobriander, i.e. to gain renown as a "master gardener".' To achieve this, he makes tremendous efforts and cultivates the biggest possible piece of gardening land. It becomes apparent, Malinowski writes, that

It has very considerable effect not only on the marriage institution itself, but on the whole economy and constitution of the tribe. Looked at from the point of view of the recipient, it is clear that every man has to guide his marital choice according to his needs, and to his prospective wife's endowment. For he will be dependent, not only on his own industry and capacity, but also on that of his relatives-in-law. A fortune-hunter will lay siege to a girl who is the only sister of several brothers – the very existence of whom would at once cool the ardor of a European with a similar end in view. Only a man who could face destitution with equanimity would court a girl who had several sisters but a single brother. As a man's wife bears sons and they grow up, he acquires as it were home-made relatives-in-law – for in a matrilineal society children are naturally classed with relatives-in-law – and their first duty is to provide for the parental household. Ordinarily the husband receives the main part of his wife's endowment from one relative-in-law only; but in the case of a chief or a man of importance, though one man will nominally be responsible, many others will co-operate with him to provide a suitable gift. Even a commoner, however, receives, besides the *urigubu* from his chief donor, a number of smaller gifts named *kovisi* or *taytupeta* from his wife's other relatives. They are all presented at harvest time and consist of several baskets of yams and other vegetables. A man also receives from his relatives-in-law various services, given as occasion demands. They have to assist him when he builds a house or canoe, arranges for a fishing expedition, or takes part in one of the public festivals. In illness, they must keep watch over him against sorcerers, or carry him to some other place where he hopes to get better. In feuds or in other emergencies he may, given certain circumstances, command their services. Finally, after his death, the bulk of mortuary duties will fall upon them. Only from time to time has the man to repay the annual services of his relatives-in-law by a gift of valuables. (pp. 125–7)

The taboo that forbids the woman's brothers, on whom the burden of the marriage gift falls, to interfere in the sister's marriage affairs only serves to cover up and rationalize the husband's and his family's actual material interests. Briefly, the facts are as follows: since the young wife's brother and all her relatives – the whole maternal clan, in fact – have to provide for the husband, the common fortune of the wife's clan is transferred to the husband. But as he is a brother himself and has on his part to provide for his sisters' husbands, the produce is continuously being transferred from one clan to another. That would be of no consequence in itself, for as the women of the husband's clan in turn marry men of the other clan, the marriage gift would flow back. The matter is complicated, however, by the fact that the clans have different ranks, and the chief, who belongs to the uppermost clan, has the right to polygamy. Therefore, the flow of marriage gifts, which otherwise would be levelled out by intermarriage, is deflected one-sidedly to the chief of one clan and his family. Before we come to a full understanding of this deflection as the beginning of the class division into oppressor and oppressed, let us see, with the help of diagrams, how, from the advantages and disadvantages that certain marriages offer, the concept of their 'lawfulness' or 'unlawfulness' is derived.

The only marriage that is considered a 'really lawful one' is the so-called *cross-cousin marriage*; that is, *marriage between the brother's son and his sister's daughter*. On the basis of Malinowski's account of the marriage gift, here are the facts as they affect the chief. First a simple diagram of a cross-cousin marriage, as shown on Figure 1 on page 73:

From this diagram we see that, in contradistinction to the 'legal' marriage, a marriage between the chief's daughter and the chief's sister's son 'is viewed with disfavour'. The diagrams following indicate the economic motives that determine these concepts – all of it based on Malinowski's account of the ritual of the marriage gift.

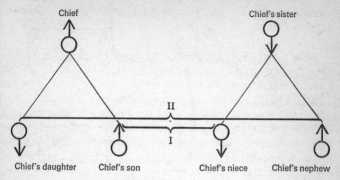

Figure 1. The 'legal' marriage (I) and the 'illegal' marriage (II), according to Malinowski. I = cross-cousin marriage

By following the arrows in the diagram on p. 74, we see clearly that only a cross-cousin marriage makes possible the accumulation of possessions and garden produce in the hands of the chief. He receives the marriage tribute from his wives' brothers, the greater part of which he has to hand on to his sister's husband. *If now his niece marries his son, the marriage tribute returns to him,* for both his nephew (sister's son and heir) and the niece's parents – that is, her father, the chief's brother-in-law – must deliver marriage tribute to his son yearly for as long as the marriage lasts. But since the son has to provide for his mother's household, in which of course the father partakes, he shares his son's economic rights.

His real legal heir is the sister's son, to whom his fortune and rank pass after his death. There is no more than a relation of friendship between father and son; as father he has the right to procure certain privileges for his son, but only during his lifetime. The chief has only one way to secure a lasting position in the village for his son, with full rights for himself and his offspring. There is only one way to insure the son's lifelong enjoyment of all gifts, and that is if the chief marries his sister's daughter to his own son. In this way the son acquires the right to live in the village and to participate in tribal affairs and magic if he so wishes. He therefore has the

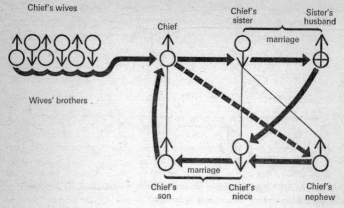

Figure 2. How the cross-cousin marriage benefits the chief by returning to him the marriage tribute he gives his brother-in-law, thus making possible the accumulation of wealth

same position after the chief's death as during his lifetime, a position he would have had to relinquish in favour of the rightful heir, the chief's sister's son,[11] had he not married the chief's niece.

As the chief can give his son as many gifts as he likes during his lifetime, the son benefits greatly from this marriage, which secures to him their permanent possession. The real heir is bound by strict taboo not to interfere with his sisters' marriage affairs. He has no influence, then, over this event, which is so

11. An analytical interpretation of the cross-cousin marriage easily offers itself: the incest taboo between brother and sister is cancelled by their children's marriage, through identification of the brother with his son and of his sister with her daughter. And the explanation offered by the primitive sounds very tempting from the point of view of this interpretation: 'Sometimes, for instance, it will be stated as a rider to the principle of exogamy that "the marriage between brother and sister is wrong" ("brother and sister" in the extended sense, all people of opposite sex and of the same generation related through the mother). "To marry a *tabula* (cross-cousin) is right; the true *tabula* (the first cross-cousin) is the proper wife for us"' (*Sexual Life of Savages*, p. 101). But the economic interests are so clear that in this instance we can allow the psychological factor only a subordinate part.

detrimental to his interests. When Malinowski writes that through this an alliance is established between the chief's son and the rightful heir, the chief's nephew, 'which frustrates the potential rivalry between them', we may presume that this is an error, for by this marriage the rightful heir takes upon himself the obligation of paying tribute to the chief's son. Let us read Malinowski himself:

The matrilineal principle is maintained by the more rigid rules of tribal law. These rules decree absolutely that a child must belong to the family, sub-clan, and clan of its mother. Less absolutely but still very strictly, they regulate the membership of a village community and the office of magician They also assign all inheritance of land, privileges and material goods to mother-line. But here a number of customs and usages allow, if not an evasion, at least a compromise and modification of tribal law. *By these usages, a father can, for his own lifetime, grant the right of citizenship in his village to his son and bestow upon him the usufruct of canoes, lands, ceremonial privileges, and magic. By cross-cousin marriage, combined with matrilocal residence, he can even secure all these things to his son for life.*

We have to note one more important difference in the transmission of material goods and privileges, as from maternal uncle to a nephew on the one hand, and a father to a son on the other. A man is obliged to relinquish all his possessions and offices to his younger brother or maternal nephew at death. But usually the younger man wants to possess some of these things during his senior's lifetime; and it is customary for a maternal uncle to part with a portion of his gardens or some of his magic while he is still living. *But in such cases the nephew must pay*, and the payment is often quite substantial. It is called by the special technical name *pokala*.

When a man gives any of these things to his son, on the other hand, he does it of his free will, and quite gratuitously. Thus, a maternal nephew, or younger brother, has the right to claim his share, and always receives it if he gives the first instalment of the *pokala*. The son relies on his father's good-will, which, as a rule, works very effectively on his behalf, and he receives all the gifts for nothing. The man who has the right to the things has to pay for them, while the man who receives them without the sanction of tribal law gets them gratis. Of course he has to return them, at least in part, after his father's death; but the use and enjoyment he has had of material benefits remain his, while the magic he cannot return.

The natives explain this anomalous state of things by the father's partiality to his children, which, in its turn, is accounted for by his relation to their mother. The natives say that his free gifts to the children are a reward for the free cohabitation which he enjoys with his wife. (pp. 208–10; Reich's italics)

It results from this that cross-cousin marriage is not, as Malinowski frequently emphasizes, 'a compromise between the two ill-adjusted principles of mother-right and father-love' (p. 101), but on the contrary an institution that increasingly strengthens father-right. If the chief's power grows continuously, one further step suffices – i.e. the legal transference of the right of inheritance from the maternal to the paternal line, from the sister's son to the chief's own son – and father-right stands before us complete. With the Trobrianders, whose right of inheritance is still organized on the principle of mother-right, we can see what privileges the chief can grant his son in his lifetime, and how by cross-cousin marriage he forcibly achieves the transference of possessions and power to his line.

Only once does Malinowski hint that patriarchal principles, not mere paternal love, are asserting themselves. That is when he writes: 'On the apparently unpropitious soil of strict matriliny, with its denial of any paternal bond through procreation and its declaration of the father's extraneousness to progeny, there spring up certain beliefs, ideas, and customary rules, which smuggle extreme patrilineal principles into the stronghold of mother-right' (pp. 203–4).

Two additional diagrams (p. 77) will make clearer still the fact that essentially it is for economic reasons that marriage between the chief's daughter and his sister's son is deemed 'not good' or 'not decent'.

In Figure 3 we assume that the niece marries some other man. In that case, we see by following the arrow, the chief cannot accumulate anything, as he hands on his possessions through his sister to his brother-in-law and his family and through his nephew, who inherits his goods, to the unrelated husband of his niece. Not only does his responsibility for his sister cause him great expense during his lifetime, but after

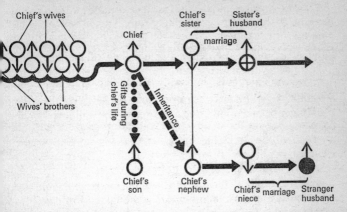

Figure 3. Economic disadvantages for the chief if his niece marries whom she will. (Arrows indicate the flow of the marriage gift)

his death his possessions change clan because his nephew has to pay the marriage tribute to his (the chief's) niece's husband, who is of a different clan.

In Figure 4 we see a situation that is even worse for the

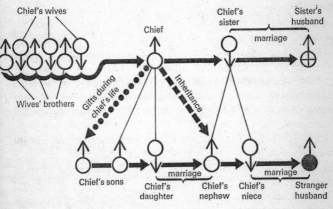

Figure 4. The 'bad' marriage (between the chief's daughter and the chief's nephew). The fortunes of the chief's sons, too, leave the chief's line

chief. In addition to the transference of his possessions along
these two lines, his sons, to whom he makes gifts during his
lifetime, also enrich his nephew through his daughter. But
the enriching of the nephew rather than of the son has no
advantage whatever for him, because the nephew does not
contribute anything to the household. This accounts for the
strained relations between uncle and nephew and the loving
relations between father and son to which Malinowski refers
time and again.

OPPRESSION AND ITS IDEOLOGICAL ANCHORING

We have seen how the institution of the marriage tribute alters
the balance of power in favour of the father and chief, how
father-right, and with it the patriarchal polygamous family,
grows out of the primeval matriarchal organization and the
kinship clans. For the chief, possibilities and rights come as a
result of his power (and of his obligations) – e.g. the right of
polygamy and the beginnings of a feudal power to command
over his wives' brothers and other relatives, who are obliged to pay tribute to him. Let us read Malinowski on the
chief of Omarakana:

The headman of Omarakana, and chief of Kiriwina is supreme in
rank, power, extent of influence and renown. His tributary grasp,
now considerably restricted by white men and crippled by the
disappearance of some villages, used to reach all over the northern
half of the island and comprise about five dozen communities,
villages, or sub-divisions of villages, which yielded him up to sixty
wives. Each of these brought him in a substantial yearly income in
yams. Her family had to fill one or two storehouses each year containing roughly five to six tons of yams. The chief would receive
from 300 to 350 tons of yams per annum. The quantity which he
disposes of is certainly sufficient to provide enormous feasts, to
pay craftsmen for making precious ornaments, to finance wars and
oversea expeditions, to hire dangerous sorcerers and assassins – to
do all, in short, which is expected of a person in power. (p. 132)

Polygamy (*vilayawa*) is allowed by custom to people of higher
rank or to those of great importance, such as, for instance, the
sorcerers of renown. In certain cases, indeed, a man is obliged to

have a great number of wives by virtue of his position. This is so with every chief, that is to say, every headman of high rank who exercises an over-rule in a more or less extended district. In order to wield his power and to fulfil the obligations of his position, he must possess wealth, and this in Trobriand social conditions is possible only through plurality of wives. (p. 130)

With a shifting of inheritance from the maternal to the paternal line, which is inevitable in such a development, the trend in society towards a system of feudalism and slavery can no longer be halted. Once the possessions, and with them the power, are concentrated in the chief's hands and family, only some progress in the means of production is required to bring about the situation Marx placed at the beginning of class society. The increasing division of labour leads to the production of goods for exchange, but the means of production are in the hands of the chief and his family, or at least it is in his power to make them his at any time – a characteristic of the onset of a definitive division into classes: those who possess the means of production, and those who do the work. When examining the legal system of the Trobrianders, we saw this clearly in an embryonic stage, a horizontal and a vertical 'relation of exploitation' – horizontally, the exploitation of the wives' brothers by the husbands; vertically, a step-like converging of power in the higher-ranking upper clans, the exploitation of the men by the chief through the women married to him. Parallel to this relationship of oppression runs a shifting of power from the maternal to the paternal line.

If we examine the roundabout methods of native economy more closely, we see that they provide a powerful incentive to industrial efficiency. If he worked just to satisfy his own immediate wants, and had only the spur of directly economic considerations, the native, who has no means of capitalizing his surplus, would have no incentive to produce it. The deep-rooted motives of ambition, honor, and moral duty, have raised him to a relatively high level of efficiency and organization which, at seasons of drought and scarcity, allows him to produce just enough to tide over the calamity. (p. 129)

The ever-present real motive is the primitive system of gain through marriage. Ambition, honour, and moral duty are themselves results of this relation between brother and sister's husband, ideological anchorings of the already oppressive economic system, which is kept alive by the marriage system and is constantly spreading. We cannot understand why Malinowski, after what he himself described, comes to the conclusion that the Trobriander is not driven by economic incentives.

The mourning rites, which Malinowski describes in detail, also tell us that this economic relation between the maternal and the paternal clan has already given rise to the ideological germs of hatred between oppressed and oppressor. On the husband's death it is not, as might be expected, his kinsmen who are obliged to express extreme grief, but his wife's relations, especially her brothers. Of the funeral festivities, Malinowski writes:

The ritual performances at his twice-opened grave and over his buried remains, and all that is done with his relics, is merely a social game, where the various groupings into which the community has re-crystallized at his death play against each other. (p. 149)

The kindred must also not display any outward signs of mourning in costume and ornamentation, though they need not conceal their grief and may show it by weeping. Here the underlying idea is that the maternal kinsmen (*veyola*) are hit in their own persons; that each one suffers because the whole sub-clan to which they belong has been maimed by the loss of one of its members. 'As if a limb were cut off, or a branch lopped from a tree.' Thus, though they need not hide their grief, they must not parade it. This abstention from outward mourning extends, not only to all the members of the sub-clan beyond the real kinsmen, but to all the members of the clan to which the dead man belonged. (pp. 150–51)

Quite different, in the native idea, is the relation of the widow, and of the children and relatives-in-law, to the dead and to his corpse. They ought, according to the moral code, to suffer and to feel bereaved. But in feeling thus they are not suffering directly; they are not grieving for a loss which affects their own sub-clan (*dala*) and therefore their own persons. Their grief is not spontaneous like that of the *veyola* (maternal kinsmen) but a duty almost artificial, springing as it does from acquired obligations. Therefore they must ostentatiously express their grief, display it, and bear witness to it by outward signs. If they did not, they would offend the surviving members of the dead man's sub-clan. Thus an interesting situation develops, giving rise to a most strange spectacle: a few hours after the death of a notable, the village is thronged by people, with their heads shaven, the whole body thickly smeared with soot, and howling like demons in despair. And these are the non-kinsmen of the dead man, the people not actually bereaved. In contrast to these a number of others are to be seen in their usual attire, outwardly calm and behaving as if nothing had happened. These represent the sub-clan and clan of the deceased, and are the actually bereaved. Thus by a devious reasoning, tradition and custom produce the reverse of what would seem natural and obvious to us or any observer from almost any other culture . . . In this group, and it may be that of the sons also, an observer well acquainted with these natives would be able to distinguish an interesting interplay of feigned and merely histrionic grief with real and heartfelt sorrow. (pp. 151–2)

After the second exhumation the body is buried, the wake is over, and the people disperse; but the widow, who, during all this time, has not stirred from her husband's side, nor eaten nor drunk nor stopped in her wailing, is not yet released. Instead she moves into a small cage, built within her house, where she will remain for months together, observing the strictest taboos. She must not leave the place; she may only speak in whispers; she must not touch food or drink with her own hands, but wait till they are put into her mouth; she remains closed up in the dark, without fresh air or light; her body is thickly smeared over with soot and grease, which will not be washed off for a long time. She satisfies all the necessities of life indoors, and the excreta have to be carried out by her relatives. Thus she lives for months shut up in a low-roofed, stuffy, pitch-dark space, so small that with out-stretched hands she can almost touch the walls on either side; it is often filled with people who assist or comfort her, and pervaded by an indescribable atmosphere of human exhalations, accumulated bodily filth, stale food, and smoke. Also she is under the more or less active control and surveillance of her husband's matrilineal relatives, who regard her mourning and its inherent privations as their due. When the term of her widowhood has almost run its course – its length depends upon the status of her husband and varies from about six months to two years – she is gradually released by the dead man's kinsmen. Food is put into her mouth according to a ritual which gives her permission to eat with her own hands. Then, ceremonially, she is allowed to speak; finally she is released from the taboo of confinement and, still with appropriate ritual, requested to walk forth. At the ceremony of her complete release by the female *veyola* of the dead man, the widow is washed and anointed, and dressed in a new gaudy grass skirt in three colours. This makes her marriageable again ... The corresponding idea, that it is the imperative duty of the widow and her relatives to show grief and perform all the mortuary services, emphasizes the strength and the permanence of marriage bonds as viewed by tradition ... In the first place, it is a duty towards the dead and towards his sub-clan, a duty strongly enjoined by the code of morals and guarded by public opinion, as well as by the kinsmen. 'Our tears – they are for the kinsmen of our father to see', as one of the mourners simple and directly told me. In the second place, it demonstrates to the world at large that the wife and children were really good to the dead and that they took great care of him in his illness. Lastly, and this is very important, it allays any suspicion of their complicity in his murder by black magic. To understand the last queer motive, one has to realize the extreme fear, the ever-vigilant suspicion of sorcery, and the unusual lack of trust in anyone at all with reference to it. The Trobrianders, in common with all races at their culture level, regard every death without exception as an act of sorcery, unless it is caused by suicide or by a visible accident, such as poisoning or a spear thrust. It is characteristic of their idea of *the bonds of marriage and fatherhood – which they regard as artificial and untrustworthy under any strain – that the principal suspicion of sorcery attaches always to the wife and children.* The real interest in a man's welfare, the real affection, the natural innocence of any attempt against him are, by the traditional system of ideas, attributed to his maternal kinsmen. His wife and children are mere strangers, and custom persists in ignoring any real identity of interest between them. (pp. 157–8, 159, 160–61; Reich's italics)

Psychoanalytic research has disclosed that a person who displays grief in an especially conspicuous way is covering up a forbidden repressed hatred. We see that the Trobrianders are suspicious of each other where they are in a mutual relation of exploitation, and that they are aware of the artificial nature of marriage. The wife's clan had been burdened and, through the death of the husband, was freed from burdens; therefore, it would have reason to rejoice. The members of the clan had built up hatred, unconsciously or consciously, for the receiver of the tribute. Now, watched suspiciously by the husband's family, they must show that they did not hate him for the burdens they had to carry but carried them willingly and gladly. The dead man's kinsmen have no material obligations to him and so they do not have to drown any hatred by a compensatory show. They are allowed to mourn in a natural way.

Here we see moral customs arising directly out of the production relationship, but we also recognize another of their functions, *the ideological fixation of the economic situation* from which they spring. It is of course entirely unknown to the Trobrianders that this ideology, which is rooted in the psychic structures of the suppressed through a change of their instinctual lives, affects the economic situation and makes permanent the material suppression of these individuals, preventing their rebellion. This function of ideology can be expected to exist wherever an ideology corresponds to a relation of oppression. We shall deal with this question in Part II.

Since at this stage in the organization of society the interest in the institution of marriage as the central mechanism of oppression is already powerful, the widow has to take upon herself the most terrible privations for a long time; she is watched suspiciously by the husband's relatives, who determine how long she has to submit to the mourning rites. This is understandable when we consider that her genitality was badly restricted by her husband and that she of necessity hated him, too. Before she can enjoy full freedom, she must show by suffering that she loved him and had not practised black magic on him. *Tout comme chez nous.*

3

The Invasion of Sex-Negative Moralism

PREMARITAL CHASTITY

WITH one exception, the genital love life of the Trobrianders before marriage not only is completely free since childhood but in addition is socially sanctioned (see Chapter 1). The one exception is those children who are destined for a cross-cousin marriage; social custom demands of them premarital chastity, and they must refrain from the otherwise usual and eagerly indulged in genital activities. Malinowski merely records this fact under the heading 'Ceremonies of Infant Betrothal' without drawing any connection.

In my investigation of the sociological function of the suppression of infantile and adolescent sexuality,[12] connections arose from the relation of private property, the marriage institution, and the demand for asceticism in youth. These are not only confirmed by Malinowski's findings, but their very origin becomes apparent through them. Let me briefly re-iterate the results of my investigation:

Our youth research maintains, wherever it comes across the problem of the asceticism of youth, that such asceticism serves the needs of 'culture', that culture and civilization are in-conceivable without an ascetic life for youth. It was natural to assume that not culture generally but only a certain form of culture considers the asceticism of youth, or at least the demand for it, an integral part of it. But how could the demand for asceticism be fitted into the sociological process?

At first, it was clear only that for some reason authoritarian society is interested in the institution of compulsive marriage. It promulgates the social protection of women, who have no rights, and of children; it establishes and economically safe-guards the right of inheritance along the paternal line, and in

12. Part I of *The Sexual Revolution*.

addition it constitutes the backbone of the authoritarian ideological factory, the patriarchal family – that being its political function in a reactionary society. This does not explain the demand for asceticism. Why should youth not live according to their bioenergetic needs, provided that later, in marriage, they acquiesce to the demands of patriarchy? The answer was suggested by the sex-economic clinic: persons who reach the full development of their genital needs, either through a special stroke of fortune or by a cure, become incapable of conforming to the monogamous demand – 'one partner for life'. A comparison with the sexually crippled and therefore armoured wives who can tolerate morality, and the relative ease with which sexually crippled men keep to monogamy, shows that: (1) *the impairment of genital sexuality makes men and women capable of marriage;* (2) *the full development of genitality through a satisfactory sex life before marriage* does not *destroy* the possibility of monogamy of a certain duration, but it does destroy the *capacity for lifelong monogamy.* Looked at objectively and without subjective rationalizations, the social purpose of the demand for asceticism in youth and for sexual suppression in early childhood is, therefore, the insuring of man's *capacity for lifelong compulsory marriage.* That is openly expressed in many publications of the church and of undisguisedly reactionary moralists.

We will not go into detail here concerning resulting contradictions in the marriage institution, but only stress this fact: private power and state power have a vested interest in the institution of compulsory marriage;[13] the latter in turn requires for its existence the strictest application of infantile and adolescent asceticism. This – and not, as a badly misinformed sex research maintains, considerations of 'culture' – is the real reason behind the demand for asceticism. It was not difficult to prove clinically, contrary to the dreary insistent reiteration that pubertal genital embrace has a harmful effect on health, that in practice this demand is not obeyed, and that conflict-laden self-satisfaction does far more damage than the genital embrace in puberty could ever do. It is guilt feelings

13. Cf. *The Sexual Revolution.*

and sexual anxiety that keep the adolescent from living a genital life. They make him impotent, incapable of gratification, and therefore, in the end, unexacting sexually in so far as his conscious life is concerned. In the process, about 60 per cent of the men and 90 per cent of the women fall ill with nervous and sexual complaints. This is not the intended result of sexual regulation, of course, but it is inherent in the system, a system that finds its supporters among so many sex researchers. Until now, psychoanalytic youth research, too, has fallen prey to this error, in spite of the facts, which speak so clearly.

Statistics on the relationship between marital faithfulness and the time when the sexual embrace begins, compiled by Barasch in Moscow, brought a confirmation: of those who started genital sexual life after their twenty-first year of life, only 17·2 per cent were unfaithful; of those who had genital sexual life between their seventeenth and twenty-first year of life, 47·6 per cent were unfaithful; and finally, among those who had started genital sexual life before they were seventeen, the percentage of marital unfaithfulness was 61·6.[14]

Morally prejudiced sex research could offer several objections to these theoretical conclusions and to the statistics. But in the otherwise sexually free Trobriand society, the demand for infantile and adolescent asceticism sets in just where the material interests are most obvious; namely, with cross-cousin marriage. This shows irrefutably the economic background of the demand for asceticism and definitely invalidates the empty claim of cultural considerations. Similarly, the love life of Trobriand youth refutes the babble about the genital embrace being harmful to health. Nobody can maintain that the Trobrianders have not reached a very high standard of horticultural society and yet they have free adolescent genital love life. Proof that the harm in active pubertal genitality springs from the social obstacles to sex life (educational sexual crippling, shortage of housing, oppressing parental home, etc.), from the contradictions between sexual and economic existence and not from any sort of natural cir-

14. M. Barasch, 'Sex Life of the Workers of Moscow', *Journal of Social Hygiene*, vol. XII, no. 5, May 1926.

cumstances, has already been given in part in 'The Fiasco of Sexual Moralism'.[15]

Let us now return to Malinowski's report on the break-in of the demand for asceticism. The mother's brother, who has a material interest, always takes the initiative in bringing about a cross-cousin marriage. As soon as a son is born to him, he approaches his sister with the request that she destine her daughter or a daughter's daughter to be that son's wife. (The age disparity should not be more than two or three years.)

Or the boy's father may wait, and if within ten years or so a girl is born to his sister, he may requisition her as a future daughter-in-law. His sister is not allowed to refuse his application. Soon after the preliminary agreement has been concluded, the man has to take a *vaygu'a* (valuable), a polished axe-blade or shell ornament, and give it to his sister's husband, the father (*tama*) of the infant bride. 'This is the *katupwoyna kapo'ula* for your child,' he says, and adds that it is given '*so that she may not sleep with men, nor make katuyausi (licentious escapades), nor sleep in the bukumatula (bachelor's house). She must sleep in her mother's house only.*' Shortly after this, three gifts of food are offered by the girl's family to the boy's father. They are similar in nature to the three initial gifts in ordinary marriage, and are designated by the same names: *katuvila*, *pepe'i*, and *kaykaboma*. (pp. 104–5; Reich's italics)

But before the two are safely married, a somewhat difficult course has to be steered. Although nobody seriously expects the young people to be chaste and faithful to each other, appearances have to be kept up. A flagrant transgression of the obligation to the betrothed would be resented by the offended party, and with some exaggeration called 'adultery.' It is considered a great shame to the girl if her fiancé openly has a liaison with someone else, and she on her side must not make a *bukumatula* her permanent abode either in the company of her betrothed or of anyone else; nor may she go to other villages on those avowedly sexual expeditions called *katuyausi*. Both parties to the betrothal must carry on their amours discreetly and *sub rosa*. This, of course, is neither easy nor pleasant for them, and they tread the straight path of superficial decorum only under heavy pressure. The boy knows what he has to lose, so he is as careful as he can bring himself to be. Also, the father controls his son to some extent, and at the same time exercises some authority

15. *The Sexual Revolution*, Part I.

over his future daughter-in-law, through his status of maternal uncle. A man who had betrothed his son and niece to each other put the matter thus to me: 'She is afraid that she might die (that is, by sorcery), or that I might hit her.' And, of course, her mother is very careful and does what she can to conceal and make light of her daughter's delinquencies. (pp. 106–7)

We see that, with suppression, clandestine activities set in; the heavy pressure of the new morality, which so grossly contradicts the otherwise free sexual organization, succeeds in making a Trobriand girl, in a society in which the beating of children is a disgrace, afraid of being beaten for sexual transgressions, and the mothers of these girls begin to develop the behaviour of our mothers. To repeat, so that no misunderstanding may arise:

At the next harvest, the girl's father brings a *vilakuria* (substantial contribution of yam food) to the boy's parents. This latter fact is interesting, since it is a reversal, on account of the anticipated marriage, of what happens in the previous generation. The boy's father, who is the brother of the girl's mother, has to give a harvest gift year by year to the girl's parents; and this at the time of his sister's marriage he had inaugurated by a gift of *vilakuria*. Now he receives on behalf of his infant son a *vilakuria* gift from his sister's husband, who acts as the representative of his own son or sons, that is the brother or brothers of the future bride, who, later on will annually bring substantial harvest offerings to the household, when it becomes such. (p. 105)

And as the sons also have to provide for their mother's household, by the backward flow of the harvest gifts to the point of origin, the circle is closed, and with that the foundation for sexual suppression is laid. We saw in the first chapters how, in a patriarchy, when this suppression assumes certain proportions, it becomes a factor that produces neuroses *en masse*.

CRUEL PUBERTY RITES

Freud has endeavoured to make the puberty rites of circumcision and genital mutilation among primitive peoples understandable to us. In his book *Negereros*, Felix Bryk describes the removal of the prepuce of boys and the excision of the clitoris and the lips of the vulva among many peoples (Egyptians, Nubians, Abyssinians, Sudanese; also Negro tribes in western Africa, the Susu, Bambuc, Mandingo, and Masai and Wakussi in east Africa, and others). According to Krische, these rites, which to him are a sign of the brutalization of sexuality and anticipated punishment for sexual activity, as Freud would say, are not characteristic of patriarchal organizations alone. He says that they were once prevalent among the Kamchadals and have been found among the matriarchal Malayans of the East Indian archipelago. According to Johann J. Bachofen, this custom also existed among the 'matriarchally-minded Egyptians'.[16] Bryk writes about the African Bantu tribes:

This excision, which is restricted to the clitoris, puts limits to the wanton activity of the girls. From being common property she becomes private property. [The African tribe described here is wholly patriarchal.] The practical importance lies in the fact that the young convalescent girl is withdrawn from the approaches of the young men for a prolonged period of time. But the primary purpose is that of restraining her wantonness by the extirpation of that organ which is most sensitive to the libido sexualis in order in this way to impose upon her monogamy which goes against her nature. (*Negereros*)

That the genital ceremonies, which as part of the puberty rites include the mutilation of the genitals and the infliction of pain, represent patriarchal society's opposition to the genitality of youth is not to be doubted. The question is: What is the socioeconomic meaning of these rites, and where do they fit historically in the development of sexual morality and sexual suppression? It is improbable that the rites date back to primeval times, when love life was free and unrestricted. *They must, therefore, have developed since*. They are virtually a characteristic of primitive patriarchal organizations, and according to Krische, they are also found in matriarchal

16. After Paul Krische, *Das Rätsel der Mutterrechtsgesellschaft*.

societies. How can this be reconciled with the sex-affirmative character of the latter?

We must consider two things. First, these rites are not frequent among matriarchally organized tribes; and the Egyptians, among whom they were found, were only 'matriarchally-minded'. Second, we must not imagine, contrary to history, that mother-right and father-right are clearly separated. Wherever mother-right passed into father-right, the transition of economic and social institutions and customs took a long time. And if we add that the sex-economic function of puberty mutilation is to suppress adolescent genitality, we must conclude that this measure arose in the *transition period*; that, in the course of the change-over from sex-affirmation to sex-negation, it established itself as an economically necessary measure. When and in what connection? We can only guess at this, as the evidence is quite insufficient. But our guess fits without difficulty into our history of sexual morality and is in complete accord with what we know of the genital apparatus.

As long as cross-cousin marriage, which is so important economically, was not fully developed, and chastity therefore was not yet demanded of the mass of youth, moral pressure was sufficient. With the spreading of the demand for chastity, sexual rebellion among the youth naturally grew and strengthened. If the whole system of 'lawful' marriages was not to be endangered, since premarital genital freedom makes people incapable of compulsory marriage, the demand for chastity had to assert itself, and stricter measures became necessary. The excision of the clitoris in girls serves the purpose of forcefully diminishing genital excitability. Excision has then, ultimately, a compulsory social function which is rooted in custom and habit and thus hidden. The operation adolescents have to undergo is not an anticipated punishment for genital activity, not a 'revengeful act' of the adults, but a rational, well-founded measure of the ruling group to suppress pubertal genitality, which is disadvantageous at this stage of economic development. Later and more mature patriarchy works in a subtler and more successful way. It fights *infantile* sexuality and from the start, through rigid armouring, impairs the sexual structure in the direction of orgastic impotence, at the same time unintentionally burdening itself with neuroses, perversions, and sexual crime. Undoubtedly, in these economic interests of budding patriarchy lie the historical roots of the castration anxiety Freud discovered in authoritarian man. And the same motives that at one time laid the foundation for man's castration complex preserve it today – viz. the interests in compulsory marriage for life, the executive agents of which are, quite unconsciously, the parents.

4

Primitive Work-Democracy[17] – Mother-Right; Private Ownership of the Means of Production – Father-Right

WE have seen father-right grow out of mother-right among the Trobrianders, and we recognized in the ritual marriage gift the basic mechanism of the transformation of the social organization. We saw the primeval work-democratic maternal clan becoming more and more dependent economically on the increasingly patriarchal chief and his family – this process being covered up ideologically. Are we dealing here with a general or at least widely prevalent type of primeval transformation into patriarchy and into class division, or does this apply only to the Trobrianders and a few other tribes? It is not easy to give a definite answer to this question. No report as accurate and detailed as Malinowski's has been presented. Either the penetrating analysis of the sex life is missing, or there is no attempt to relate sexual and economic conditions, so

17. In the German edition of this book published in 1931, the term *primeval communism* was used to describe the economic functioning of original matriarchal primitive society. However, the complete misuse and prostitution of the word *communism* by red fascism over the past decades has made the term *primeval communism* misleading and unusable. For this reason, and in accordance with the development of the *sex-political* sociology of 1931 into the *orgonomic* sociology of 1951, the term *work-democracy* is hereafter substituted for *primeval communism*, save in those instances where the author is quoting from or referring to the work of others who used the term *primeval communism*. *Work-democracy* is defined as the natural and intrinsically rational work relationships between human beings. The concept of *work-democracy* represents the *reality* (not the ideology) of these relationships, which, though usually distorted because of the prevalent biological armouring and irrational ideologies, are nevertheless at the basis of all social achievement. *Work-democracy excludes all forms of dictatorial work*, and dictatorship, in turn, excludes work-democratic functioning.

that no satisfactory conclusions can be drawn. Moreover, many ethnologists believe in the priority of patriarchy, which rules out a historical, developmental viewpoint from the start. Most reports do not even indicate whether the tribes observed are organized according to father-right or mother-right; whether they are work-democratic or have an organization based on the private ownership of the means of production. Only a few ethnologists can be mentioned whose investigations offer an insight into the historical development of primeval society. Among these, Lewis Morgan,[18] in particular, followed by Engels in his book *The Origin of the Family*, upheld the primacy of mother-right. Before them, Bachofen[19] had already demonstrated that mother-right generally was the original form of organization, for it represents real *nature-right*, whereas patriarchy presupposes complicated influences of a socio-historical nature.

The data presented by the opponents of this point of view, the supporters of the primacy of patriliny, are open to various interpretations; they lack the coherence of the mother-nature-right theory and prove nothing, even if father-right is found among very primitive tribes. For this latter finding alone does not constitute proof of the primary nature of the existing organization. To take an example, although the pygmies, who are on a very low level, have a patriarchal organization,[20] their monogamy and their strictly organized incest taboo indicate a long historical development. Only a precise investigation of their folklore and myths could throw light on the question.

That mother-right should have developed out of a primary patriarchy is scarcely probable. We must consider that mother-right is characterized by primeval work-democracy and the most extensive sexual freedom. Father-right, on the other hand, wherever it is encountered, is characterized by private ownership, enslavement of women, and sexual sup-

18. *Ancient Society.*

19. *The Mother Right* (1861).

20. Cf. Roheim, 'Urformen und Wandlungen der Ehe' in Marcuse's *Ehebuch*, p. 33 ff.

pression similar to our own. The former, therefore, is much closer to the natural order. We should have to assume improperly that the development occurred in *reverse* if we wanted to derive mother-right from father-right, for this would entail the transformation of a highly complicated organization into a more primitive, more natural one. Thereby, all historical premises would be invalidated.

The third possibility, that primary father-right existed side by side with primary mother-right, is no more probable. Whereas mother-right is understandable from the natural sequence of generations and is in harmony with the facts of incest and primitive work-democracy in the earliest times, the assumption of the primacy of father-right requires highly complicated, forced hypotheses. For this assumption one usually draws upon the strength of the male, his jealousy of the other, younger or weaker (?) males, and one derives analogies from animal life, where a 'paternal' figure leads the horde. Here, the following difficulties exist: the assumption of jealousy rules out the irrefutable fact of incest in primeval times and also of economic primeval work-democracy, for if there is a strong, jealous male in a horde who claims all females for himself and excludes or drives away the other males, it must always have been so; nothing else makes sense. The excluded, embattled men could not co-operate in the primitive economy, for in so doing they would come into contact with the women; also, they could not share in the produce. It seems quite impossible, moreover, that the primeval father figure could fend off any number of equally strong men for any length of time. The only hypothetical basis for this view is the supposed jealousy of the leader and the rare occurrence of animal hordes (wild horses, stags, monkeys) in which there is a 'leader'. These biological proofs, which again and again are taken from the animal world, are insignificant in comparison with the well-established fact that millions of other kinds of animals live a promiscuous sex life, with the exception of occasional matings in the breeding season. Nevertheless, these facts are cited again and again to support patriarchal ideology.

The patriarchal concept of primeval history has also quite logically led to the assumption that compulsory monogamy (or the present-day privilege of the man to have several women), jealousy, the suppression of women, etc. have a biological foundation. If we add that this concept serves the purpose of justifying our patriarchal organization and forms part of the basis of fascist sexual ideology, whereas the matriarchal theory shows that all is subject to change and also that things can be done differently, we can hardly hesitate in deciding which concept to make our own.

The matriarchal theory is particularly helpful in explaining social facts and processes, whereas the patriarchal concept makes eternal that which is in fact constantly changing. If, thus, we assume that there was a gradual, general transition from mother-right to father-right, we find ourselves in harmony with a whole series of observed facts. We can then dispense with extreme interpretations and make clear strides in our knowledge of the history of the forms of genitality and sexual economy.

In 1927 Krische published a compilation of pertinent ethnologic data on the wide prevalence of mother-right both historically and in the present-day.[21] The difficult task remains of demonstrating in detail how father-right developed out of mother-right in individual primitive organizations, as we have demonstrated was the case with the Trobrianders. Mother-right has been found: (1) among the agricultural Indians of North America – the Missouri tribes, the Iroquois, the Hurons, the Algonquin tribes, the Muskogee, Choctaws, and Cherokees, the Natchez, the Pueblos; among the primitive peoples of South America – the Tupi, the Caribbees and Arawaks; (2) in the East among the Malayan tribes, the Nicobar and Pelew Islanders, among the tribes on Formosa; matriarchal, primeval tribes in China and in India (the Garos, Pani-Kooch, and Kulu); (3) in the ancient cultures – in Athens, Sparta, Megara, Crete, Lemnos, Lesbos, Samothrace, Elis, Mantinea, Lykea, Kyria; in Rome; also among the Arabs, the Tibetans, the Celts, the Slavs, etc.

21. *Das Rätsel der Mutterrechtsgesellschaft.*

A fundamental theory on the interrelation of economic primeval work-democracy and mother-right can be found only in Morgan, who first showed that they were universally prevalent in primeval society. Roheim made a study of the tribes that have a primeval work-democratic organization,[22] without, however, relating their economic systems to their laws of lineage. The common features are these: common ownership of ground and huts, common work and distribution of produce, private ownership only of tools, ornaments, clothes, etc. – as, for instance, among the Kulis, the Lengua Indians, the Eskimos, the primeval inhabitants of Brazil, the Bakairi, the inhabitants of Australia generally, those of Tasmania; among the Comanches, the Sioux Indians, the Indo-Chinese peoples, primitives on the Solomon Islands. Sometimes, however, the hunting grounds of alien tribes are strictly divided off and trespassing leads to war.

One of Roheim's statements directs us to our central problem, the mechanism of the marriage gift. Roheim maintains that among many tribes property is equivalent to an erotic bond, and as proof he mentions the fact that in certain ceremonies the wives represent landed property. If it is true that the marriage gift passes through the wife into the husband's and his clan's ownership – for the clans concerned are exogamous – we can understand this ceremony of eroticizing symbolism: *property is transferred by means of sexual interests*. Roheim states that among various tribes with primitive work-democracy the owner's relationship to his 'property' has more a formal and ceremonial than a practical nature. We learn the same from Malinowski concerning canoe ownership among the Trobrianders.

Through these and similar findings of ethnologic investigators, which correspond to conditions among the Trobrianders, the marriage gift assumes a more general significance. It is, as we have seen, the basic mechanism of the transition from mother-right to father-right, from primeval, tribal work-democracy to the accumulation of wealth in one

22. Roheim, *Die Urformen und der Ursprung des Eigentums*, Archiv für Ethnographie, Bd. 28, H. 1/2.

family, and consequently from original sex-affirmation to sexual suppression. However, keeping all this in mind, future research among other tribes and primitive peoples will have to show how prevalent the custom is and with what frequency it has transformed matriarchal organizations into patriarchal ones.

Should this transition be found to apply generally, marriage and the marriage gift would emerge as a sociological mechanism which in primeval society, at the onset of class division, creates a relationship of exploitation in much the same way as the buying of the commodity 'working power' constitutes the mechanism of capitalist accumulation in our society.

THE MARRIAGE GIFT AS A PRELIMINARY STEP TOWARDS MERCHANDISING

If the sex-negating morality that replaces the original sex-economic regulation of love life springs from definite economic interests, we must take a look at the nature of this economic change. It is twofold. There is, first, an improvement in production techniques, which leads to greater wealth in the society; and second, a division of labour, which is closely tied up with it and substitutes the production of commodities for production for one's personal use.

The division of labour in society, and the corresponding restriction of individuals to particular occupations, arises, like the division of labour in manufacture, from contraposed starting-points. Within a family, and, after further development, within a tribe, there occurs a spontaneous division of labour in accordance with differences in sex and age, a division therefore based on a purely physiological foundation. The material subjected to this division of labour expands proportionally with the extension of the community, with the increase of population, and above all thanks to conflicts between different tribes and the subjugation of one tribe by another. On the other hand . . . an exchange of products originates at points where different families, tribes, or communities come into contact – for, in the early stage of civilisation, the independent units that confront one another are not private individuals, but families, tribes, etc. Different communities discover in their natural environment different means of production and different means of subsistence. Consequently their methods of production, modes of life, and products, are different. It is owing to the existence of these spontaneously developed differences that, when communities come into contact, there occurs an exchange of their several products one for another, so that these products gradually become transformed into commodities. Exchange does not create the difference between the spheres of production: it brings the differing spheres of production into relation one with another, and thus transforms them into more or less interdependent branches of a social collective production. Thus the social division of labour originates through exchange between spheres of production that are primarily distinct from and independent of one another. But where the physiological division of labour is the starting-point, the special organs of a directly interdependent whole break away from one another, decompose (the exchange of commodities with alien communities giving the main impetus towards this process of decomposition), and they then become independent to such an extent that a connexion between the various kinds of work is kept up only by the exchange of products as commodities. In the one case what was formerly independent has become dependent, whereas in the other case what was formerly dependent has become independent.[23]

We must distinguish, then, between the exchange *within* the tribe and the exchange *between* different communities or tribes. The exchange within the tribe, which turns the dependent into the independent and vice versa, is found among the Trobrianders in a very primitive form as an exchange of marriage gifts of garden produce. It is not possible to tell from Malinowski's report whether *different* garden produce is exchanged; that is, whether this is already an actual exchange of commodities. But it is obvious that the Trobriander's production, partly for his own and his family's use and partly – the greater part – for the marriage gift, is an embryonic form of the exchange of commodities. The marriage gift would thus be a preliminary to merchandise, developing

23. Marx, *Capital*, Everyman's Library, vol. 1, pp. 370–71.

from the most primitive conditions of production, between the woman's husband and brother. We shall see later that Marx's assumption that the exchange of commodities starts with the meeting of different tribes is correct, for the exchange within the tribe between one clan and another dates back originally to the meeting of two primeval clans. But it is clear and should not be overlooked that we are dealing here not with merchandise in the full sense of the word but with its preliminary, the marriage gift, which of necessity leads first to the accumulation of wealth in one family and then to a fully developed exchange of commodities.

DEVELOPMENT OF THE PATRIARCHAL GREAT-FAMILY AND OF CLASSES

A further effect of the mechanism of the marriage gift is the development of the patriarchal great-family, such as has been described by Morgan, Engels, Cunow,[24] Lippert, Müller-Lyer,[25] and others.

Cunow writes:

The more distinctly the patriarchal great-family develops, the more strongly it finds itself in opposition to the totem community of the clan. *The heads of families appropriate one after another of the functions which formerly the clan community had the right to exercise.* From the land held in common by the totem community the landed property of the great-family emerges, while at the same time the former claims of the members of the clan to inherit the possessions of a deceased are increasingly restricted in favour of the members of his household, represented by their head, the family patriarch. Moreover the latter takes over to an increasing extent the judicial functions which formerly were exercised by the totality of the members of the totem.

On the other hand, the rise of a caste of nobility from the chiefs of the totem, the incipient division of the formerly equal members of the clan into rich and poor (according to whether they belong to rich or poor great-families), the development of special pro-

24. Heinrich Cunow, *Zur Urgeschichte der Ehe und Familie*, Ergänzungsheft der Neuen Zeit, no. 14, 1912/13.

25. Müller-Lyer, *Die Familie*, 2nd ed., 1918.

fessions, and the introduction of prisoners of war and slaves, which they bought, from foreign tribes, increasingly lead to the disintegration and finally the breaking up of the constitution of the old consanguine community. The old kinship organization which rested on blood relationship is replaced by a seignorial or state organization which rests upon class distinctions. (*Zur Urgeschichte,* p. 45)

The link between the development of different forms of sexuality and the economic premises conditioning them has been formulated for primeval society by Engels:

The less work is developed and the more restricted the quantity of its products and consequently also the wealth of society, the more prevalently the social order seems to be dominated by bonds of kinship. But under this structure of society, which is based on bonds of kinship, the productivity of work increasingly develops and with it private ownership and exchange, differences in wealth and the usefulness of foreign working power; and so the foundation for class conflicts is laid. These new social elements in the course of generations strive to adapt the old order of society to the new conditions until at last the incompatibility of the two brings about a complete revolution. The old society which is based on bonds of kinship is broken in the clash of the newly developed social classes; a new society takes its place which is held together by the state, the subdivisions of which are no longer kinship groups but alliances formed by the inhabitants of the same town or village. In this society the family order is completely dominated by the system of ownership and now all those class conflicts and class wars freely develop which form the contents of all the history written so far. (*The Origin of the Family*)

Through the growth of work productivity and the exchange of wealth, differences in wealth and the usefulness of foreign working power develop at the same time, and in this way the foundation for class conflicts is laid. The explanation for all this lies in the economic function of the marriage gift.

Others have mentioned the shifting of rights in favour of the chief, but either they make no comment or they offer a hypothetical explanation. Thus, Müller-Lyer writes that after wealth has increased, the men, mainly traders, artisans, and technicians, know how to arrange matters so that the property they acquire by work, trading, or war becomes their private property. Because of this and through the introduction of the advantageous custom of buying the woman from her family, mother-right is undermined by father-right. The sequence of events was this: Wealth increased and came into the possession of the man; this led to marriage by purchase, which turned the woman into the man's servant. Matriliny gave way to father-right; the maternal clan, to the paternal one. Succession in the family took the place of succession in the clan. This hypothesis does not show *how* wealth got into the man's hands, however; it does not indicate the mechanism behind the historical process.

Morgan writes: 'When property began to be created in masses, and the desire for its transmission to children had changed descent from the female line to the male, a real foundation for paternal power was for the first time established.' (*Ancient Society*, p. 478)

But the desire to transmit property to children itself requires an explanation. The process among the Trobrianders indicates that this desire is explained by the *material* interests of the chief or the father, who must obtain compensation for his tribute to his sister's husband. He can only do so, as we learned, through a cross-cousin marriage, which returns the marriage gift to him. Morgan goes on to say (p. 485) that the increase in property and the desire to pass it on to one's children was the motive power that brought about monogamy. That is quite true, but the desire for inheritance to pass from father to son itself is a product of the chief's material ascendancy, which as a result of his right to polygamy and of cross-cousin marriage, continuously increases. The enslavement of the lower citizens arises from this ascendancy.

The general increase in wealth can be attributed to the steady improvement of primitive techniques of food production. But this does not account for the accumulation of wealth in one family and the emergence of two classes, one growing poorer and poorer and the other ever enriching itself, the maternal clans on the one hand and the chief's family on the other. Primitive work-democracy, if for a moment we abstract from it exogamy and the mechanism of marriage, would have achieved increasing wealth without the possessions accumulating in the hands of the chief and his family. It is the transference of the marriage tribute, in the form of produce, along the brother-husband line, and the classification of the clans according to rank, that leads to this division.

But this does not happen immediately. It comes about after several changes in the means of production, following the introduction of the tribute mechanism, which we shall deal with later. Only when production has reached a certain level do objects for personal use acquire an exchange value; that is, become merchandise.

The first step by which a useful object is enabled to become an exchange-value is that it should have an existence as something which has not a use-value for its owner; and this happens when it forms a superfluous portion of some article that satisfies his immediate wants. Objects in and by themselves exist apart from man, and are therefore alienable by him. If this alienation of objects is to be reciprocal, all that is requisite is that human beings shall tacitly confront one another as the individual owners of such alienable objects, and shall thus confront one another as mutually independent persons. (Marx, *Capital*, pp. 62–3)

We see among the Trobrianders that all the brothers have to produce a surplus over and above what they need for themselves, and the chief accumulates the greater part of this surplus. He is the first who begins to consider himself a private owner and to appear as such, both to the other members of the tribe and to other chiefs. The exchange of goods with other tribes contributes greatly to this process: it eventually becomes an important incentive to the desire to accumulate wealth, which in turn intensifies the interest in 'legal' marriage.

But no such relation of mutual independence exists for the members of a primitive community, whether this take the form of a patriarchal family, or that of an ancient Indian commune, or that of the Inca State of Peru, etc. Commodity exchange begins where community life ends; begins at the point of contact between a community and an alien community, or between the members of two different communities. (p. 63)

Here we have a seeming contradiction. Marx started from the supposition that the communes were originally self-contained primeval communities. But when we find a very primitive system of exchange within these tribes, we can draw the conclusion that even they are not primeval but have come into being through the alliance of different primeval tribes. And this is correct. *These tribes have a composite structure, and when they were formed, the preliminary to the exchange of commodities, the marriage gift, originated.* This, however, requires ethnologic proof (cf. chapter 6).

Now we can see that Engels was on the right track when he said that the *origin of class division was the conflict between man and woman.* Actually the woman belongs to the oppressed clan, the man to the oppressing one, and the marriage gift sets in motion all the processes that enslave the woman and bring her family, the maternal clan, under the chief's power. Thus, taken as groups, *the first classes are the maternal and the paternal clan; looked at vertically, all the maternal clans come together on one side, and the chief's family on the other.*

During the period of transition from mother-right to father-right, the man receives the marriage gift. Once patriarchy is fully developed and all privileges and inheritance have passed to the father–son line, the marriage gift from woman to man loses its meaning and the situation is reversed: a man who wants to marry a woman now has to buy her from her father with work or work products. Since now, under patriarchal authority, the woman herself becomes an object of economic value to her father, the buying of women, which is typical of the primitive stages of patriarchy, begins, and with it the marrying of women out of their clans into those of their husbands (*enuptio gentis,* among the Romans). The marriage gift of the transition-to-patriarchy period re-emerges on a higher level in later patriarchal society in the form of the woman's 'dowry'. This change from the buying of the woman to the buying of the man calls for a special explanation, which we cannot go into here. The stealing of women in primeval times was not the immediate step before the buying of women. It goes back rather to a much earlier period of development characterized by the clash of still endogamous, alien hordes (cf. chapter 6).

5

Confirmation and Revisions of the Morgan–
Engels Theory

To form a basic notion of the process of development of the
Trobrianders, we earlier discussed the broad outlines of the
three fundamental ethnologic theories of the history of
primeval society: (1) father-right develops out of mother-
right; (2) mother-right is a late development or is accidental;
(3) father-right and mother-right originally exist side by side.
We see that the development of the Trobrianders fits in with
the concept of matriliny to father-right, and with that concept
only. Now we must go into the Morgan–Engels theory in
detail, for their discoveries about the relationship of mother-
right and patriarchy and the development of the family and of
private ownership, and their views about these, are splendidly
confirmed by Malinowski's investigations (except for a few
necessary revisions). Also, as a result of the discovery of the
marriage-gift practice among the Trobrianders and its trans-
forming economic effect on society, which has been demonstrated here, it provides a comprehensive concept of primeval
history in the face of which the prevalent, and highly contradictory, theories can make even less of a stand today than at
the time of the promulgation of Morgan's and Engels's
theses. Yet, just as the psychoanalytic ethnologist Roheim
confirms economic primeval work-democracy but, for the
sake of the tottering hypothesis of the patriarchal primeval
horde, which is upheld at all costs, does not go into its
relationship to the development of forms of sexuality, so
Malinowski overlooks the consequences of his discoveries and
the fact that they confirm Morgan's.

On comparing the results of Malinowski's investigations
with Morgan's and Engels's findings, we stumble on a major
difficulty (although otherwise there is surprising conformity):
neither Morgan nor Engels describes or even mentions a

marriage gift from the mother's brother (in the woman's clan) to his sister's husband (in the husband's family), except for a few vague remarks that might be interpreted as indicating their awareness of it. We recognized in the marriage gift the central economic mechanism of the social transformation of mother-right into father-right among the Trobrianders; moreover, the transition from matriarchy to patriarchy was found by Morgan to be quite general, and by Engels to be actually analogous, down to the smallest details, to the process among the Trobrianders. Thus, there are only two possibilities: either this mechanism applies only to Trobriand society and is not found elsewhere, or it is generally prevalent but was overlooked. The question is quite important. If the marriage gift as found among the Trobrianders is the *first* embryonic social economic relationship setting into motion the development of classes and of sex-negating morality, this fact is of no slight significance both for the understanding of primeval history and for the definitive confirmation of the theory of mother-right and the comprehension of natural sex-economy.

SUMMARY OF THE FINDINGS OF MORGAN AND ENGELS

Let us briefly sum up Morgan's and Engels's basic findings before we establish the connection between Malinowski's and our own premises and their theory.

Morgan, who spent the greater part of his life among the Iroquois Indians, was the first to discern the development of the present-day family from preliminary stages; moreover, he established that primitive peoples everywhere were organized in *Gentes* (i.e. clans) with inheritance originally along the mother-line (natural matriliny or 'mother-right'). Before him, Bachofen (in 1861) had derived his theory of original 'mother-right' from Greek and Roman mythology. Bachofen's theory postulates: (1) Unfettered sexual intercourse in primeval times; so-called hetaerism. (2) Uncertain paternity; therefore, descent along the female line. (3) Privileged position of women (gynecocracy). (4) Transition to monogamy through infringement of an age-old religious commandment that all men have claim to one and the same woman; the price paid for this infringement was that wives were shared from time to time, to a limited extent, with other men (sacred prostitution).

Engels remarks that Bachofen's derivation of father-right from mother-right is historically true but incorrect inasmuch as it supposes this transition to be due to a religious development.

In contrast to the English investigator J. F. McLennan, who in 1876 published his *Studies in Ancient History*, in which he distinguishes two primeval forms of human organization, 'exogamous' and 'endogamous' tribes, Morgan found the Iroquois organized in *endogamous tribes* consisting of *exogamous clans*. In these matriarchally organized clans, within which mating was forbidden, Morgan saw the primeval form from which the patriarchally organized clans of the Romans and Greeks later developed. Wherever the clan was found, matriarchal organizations or traces of them could be found too. This was so among the aborigines of Australia, of whom, for example, those on Mount Gambier were organized in one tribe consisting of two clans (kroki and kumite); among the Kamilaori on the Darling River in New South Wales (originally two, later six clans); among the Iroquois and all American Indians. McLennan, who had not grasped the difference between clan and tribe, found the clan organization among the Kalmucks, the Circassians, and the Samoyeds; in India among the Warelis, the Magals, the Munnipuris. Kovalewski found it among the Pschavs, the Shefzurs, the Svanetes, and other Caucasian peoples; also among the Celts and Teutons (organized, according to Caesar, *gentibus cognationibusque*). In Scotland and Ireland, clan organization existed until the eighteenth century. Besides Morgan, Arthur Wright too found it among the Seneca Iroquois. The Greeks and the Romans, however, came into history with patriarchally organized clans (*gens, genos*), which join into phratries and tribes and only gradually give way to the Greek state constitution along individual family lines. According to Bede, clan organization with female inheritance existed among the Picts. Engels derives the *fora* (i.e. gens, clan) among the Lombards and the Burgundians from *faran* (i.e. migrate), which is in complete harmony with the nomadic way of life of the primeval horde (natural right and kinship).

If we add all the earlier tribes mentioned, among whom, according to Roheim, primeval work-democracy has been found, and consider that economic primeval work-democracy in the long run rules out intimate family organization and is found always with clan organization; if, further, we keep in mind that exogamy applies always to the whole clan, never to individual families; then, even if for the moment we disregard other factors, we get a picture of universal primary clan organization, with matriliny, primeval work-democracy, exogamy in the clan, and endogamy in the tribe, which supplants the concept of a single family, either monogamous or polygamous, as the first form of organization.

According to Morgan, the development of the family parallels the development from the primeval horde to the maternal clan, to the patriarchal clan, to the patriarchal great-family, and finally to patriarchy itself. First comes the *consanguine family* (the parents' generation, the brother–sister generation and their children, each having genital satisfaction with one another); then the *punaluan family* (brothers and sisters excluded from genital embrace, but several sisters married to several brothers of another clan); then the *pairing family*, such as we still find among the Trobrianders (single pairing for a limited period of time), and eventually the lasting compulsory monogamous family of final patriarchy.

Each of the three stages in the development of mankind distinguished by Morgan – savagery, barbarism, and civilization – corresponds to a different stage of the family: consanguine family, savagery; punaluan and pairing families, barbarism; monogamous family, patriarchy and civilization. When Bachofen writes of incestuous procreation, and Caesar says of the Britons: 'Groups of ten and twelve of them have their wives in common, i.e. mostly brothers with brothers and parents with children' – 'this,' writes Engels, 'is most typical of the Punaluan family.'

The chief's polygamy, which some ethnologists place at the beginning of human development, is thus a feature of late matriarchy already on the way to becoming patriarchy. This is the stage found among the Trobrianders. It is the stage of the pairing family.

Except for the marriage gift, the following uniform structure, which corresponds fully to that of the Trobrianders, has been found wherever clan organization has been thoroughly studied:

1. Two (aborigines of Australia) to eight (Iroquois) clans matriarchally or patriarchally (depending on the stage of development of the social organization) united into tribes.

2. Clan or tribe distinguished by language, custom, and mythology. (Only rarely is there a difference from tribe to tribe. Among the Trobrianders it is *one* clan, *one* origin, *one* magic, *one* garden, *one* rank, etc.)

3. Chief's son excluded from inheritance. Instead, the sister's son or the younger brother (as, for example, among the Seneca Indians, according to Morgan) is the rightful heir to title and possessions.

4. The chief of the tribe (in some places, of the clan) can, in purely matriarchal organizations, be forced to abdicate and has the right of polygamy. The custom of choosing the chief from different clans gradually gives way to election from one and the same clan, which eventually turns into the hereditary usurpation of the chieftainship (a step towards patriarchal power).

Thus, according to Morgan, the chieftainship among the Iroquois, while remaining in the same clan, passed to the sister's son or to the younger brother. 'The fact that among the patriarchal Greeks,' writes Engels, 'the office of Basileus (military chief) passed as a rule to the son merely proves that the sons had the probability of being elected successors by people's vote, but on no account does it prove that there was legal succession without popular vote.' This, Engels remarks, was, among the Iroquois and the Greeks, the first step towards special noble families within the clan, and among the Greeks, in addition, the first step towards a future hereditary leadership, monarchy. We can follow this process among the Trobrianders just as Engels described it: the chief tries in every way possible (gifts to his son during his lifetime, matrilocal marriage for his son, the contracting of a cross-cousin marriage) to exclude the rightful heir, to an ever-increasing extent, and to put his own son in his place. The motive for this is the material advantages the chief himself enjoys through his son's privileged position; for the son has to provide for his mother's household, and the marriage gift the chief supplies to his sister returns to him in this way.

First of all, the chief can abdicate, as among the Greeks. He is the leader but has no real power to rule. This, in the words of Marx, is merely a case of 'military democracy'. But once wealth has accumulated in his family, and possibilities for exercising power have thereby emerged, then the next step, the actual transition to patriarchy through father–son inheritance, follows: chief to chief's son. Thus, Engels's view that father-right first favours the accumulation of riches in the family through the inheritance of wealth by the children and then brings about a change in its composition in the direction of a hereditary nobility and the enslavement of the members of the tribe and clan (pp. 103 ff.) requires a correction, which we derive from conditions found among the Trobrianders. The tributary obligation of the members of the tribe to the chief exists before patriarchy. It is this obligation that leads to the accumulation of wealth in the chief's family and through it to the establishment of patriarchy. The tributary duty consists, on the one hand, of the wife's brother's marriage gift to her husband, or, more specifically, the marriage gifts from the chief's wives' brothers, from several clans, to the chief. It also involves the marriage gifts from his sisters' sons, i.e. his heirs, to their sisters if the sisters marry his sons in cross-cousin marriage. In this way the one clan becomes subject to the other, and all the lesser clans become subject to the chief's and his family's. The marriage gift at this stage exists, it is true, without official sanctions. If a member of the clan does not meet his obligations, there is no forcible collection, no punishment; only his reputation suffers. The paying of tribute is guaranteed solely by custom. It is in the final stage, in the patriarchy, that legal sanctions appear in the form of forcible collection. Only then can one speak of enslavement. Thus, Tacitus speaks of the 'slaves' of the Germans, 'who pay tribute'. Just as among the Trobrianders every citizen endeavours to give handsome marriage gifts in honour of the chief, so the heads of the German clans, the *principes*, lived partly on 'gifts of honour' from members of the tribe.

Tacitus stresses the especially intimate relationship, among the Germans, between the mother's brother and his nephew. When, for instance, hostages were demanded, the nephew (sister's son), who was a member of the clan, was more highly valued than the son, who was of a different clan. Because these conditions correspond to those found among the Trobrianders, who have been studied in such detail, we may conclude the existence of other institutions, such as the marriage gift or some related practice, not mentioned by Tacitus. As long as there is no evidence to the contrary, and the clan organization of most of the tribes studied in depth shows such exact uniformity, this assumption is not only permissible but mandatory.

If, moreover, we now gather together all the scattered allusions in Morgan and Engels, as well as in Krische's study, the assumption that the marriage gift is not solely a Trobriand institution is amply confirmed.

EXISTENCE OF THE MARRIAGE GIFT IN CLAN SOCIETY

Engels writes of the Irish clan ('sept') that the land, until clan land became a domain of the king, was the common property of the clan, 'in so far as it had not already been transformed by the chiefs into their private demesne.' That shows us a two-way process of development towards patriarchy and the subjugation of the members of the clan: one that is introduced from without, by foreign tribes or peoples, and another that is operative from within. But how does the latter originate? Because of the incompleteness of the data, it is necessary to consider similar institutions jointly, even if they are found among different tribes, provided that clan organization and the brother-sister-sister's son relationship have been ascertained for all of them. And that is the case here. Among the Welsh Celts, pairing marriage still existed in the eleventh century as it was found by Malinowski among the Trobrianders in the twentieth century. When a marriage was dissolved, the woman divided the goods, and the man chose his part. If the man dissolved the marriage, he had to return the wife's dowry to her, along with other goods. If it was the woman who dissolved the marriage, she received less. Among the Trobrianders, the payment of the marriage gift ceases upon the severing of a marriage. Consequently, the man and his family, but not the woman's, are interested in preserving the marriage. Now, since among the Celts the woman brought the dowry – it is not mentioned whether it is a gift made once or a lasting obligation on her family – we are justified in drawing the conclusion that the institution of the marriage gift from the woman's clan to the man's existed. About the matriarchally organized Nicobar Islands in the Indian Ocean, south of the Andamans, Vogel writes, according to Krische: 'The women are very highly respected, and the girls have the right to turn down unpleasant suitors.' That can only be the case, of course, if it is the woman who brings the material advantages of marriage to the man. In incipient patriarchy, where the woman is bought, such a right is no longer hers. Further: 'the women enjoy complete freedom, they go about freely like the men, and as mothers they possess the respect and love of their children.' 'Vogel's report that the girls receive a dowry,' writes Krische, 'means, I suppose, that the young couples are allotted pigs, coconuts, and pandanus trees by the mother's clan.' In other words, clearly, a marriage gift from the woman's clan to the man's family is customary.

Ratzel, Grosse, and Cunow's report on the matriarchal islanders of the Carolines shows to what a great extent clan organization among the most different peoples coincides even in details, a fact that allows us to conclude that the marriage gift exists even if it is not mentioned or is only hinted at. It is shameful among these people to show that the husband has an intimate relationship with his wife, just as it is among the Trobrianders. Moreover, as among the Trobrianders, there exists the institution of the men's clubhouse, which was given this name by Ratzel (*Bai*, doubtless the same as the Trobrianders' *bukumatula*), to which the girls move at maturity; there is also matriliny.

Le Bon writes about the Garos of Assam (north of Burma, east India) that the women once wielded the supreme power in each tribe. Now this is exercised by the 'Laskar', a man 'who is usually chosen from among the richest slave-owners but who always requires the women's consent and remains subject to their advice.' Thus, once again we have a clear transition to patriarchy: rich chief, but still women's voting power. According to Ratzel, it is customary among the Garos for the bride's parents to make the marriage contract. This allows two interpretations: either the bride is bought by the man, in which case patriarchal bought-marriage already exists, or the woman's parents are interested in her marriage, as among the Trobrianders, because through the marriage they take on the obligation of making gifts to the husband. In any case, the mechanism of the marriage gift is there, and to judge from other instances, it is unlikely to diverge essentially from that of the Trobrianders. But we will not make any conclusive statement about this.

Very important for our demonstration of the widespread existence of the practice of the marriage gift is a passage from Engels regarding the Greek clan:

At the time when the Greeks enter in to history they are standing on the threshold of civilization; between them and the American tribes which were discussed above there lie two very long periods of development . . . The clan of the Greeks, therefore, is no longer the archaic one of the Iroquois, the signs of group-marriage are definitely beginning to disappear. Mother-right has given way to father-right. As after the introduction of father-right the fortune of a rich heiress would have become her husband's through the marriage, consequently another clan's, the basis of all clan law was broken through and the girl was not only allowed but in this case forced to marry inside the clan in order to preserve the fortune for it. (*The Origin of the Family*)

That should be clearly understood: the woman brought the dowry to the marriage, and as her husband was of a different clan, at the time of complete mother-right the fortune was transferred from the woman's clan to her husband's. Only father-right, having originated through the mechanism of the marriage gift, has the power to render this process harmless, which would now of necessity work to its own detriment, as in the past it had worked to its advantage. This is achieved through infringement of clan exogamy. We have seen that, except for this possibility, the custom develops among already patriarchal tribes for the man to buy the woman, whereby the marriage gift goes in the reverse direction and once and for all enslaves the woman. Through marriage, she now brings her father material advantages.

THE MARRIAGE CLASSES OF THE AUSTRALIAN ABORIGINES

Among the Trobrianders we have found the institution of 'legal' marriage in the form of cross-cousin marriage, which in this tribe is a means of compensating for the burden of the brother's (and his clan's) marriage gift to his sister's husband (and his family): his son must marry his niece (sister's daughter) so that the marriage gift may at least in part return to him. We have seen, moreover, that this marriage arrangement, originally a compensation for the tribute, changes in the case of the chief, who has the privilege of polygamy, into a mechanism for the accumulation of property in his embryonic patriarchal family. We are no longer dealing with a mere mechanism of *alleviation* for him in so far as he is a brother, but with more than that, with a mechanism of *enrichment* in so far as he is a father and an incipient patriarch. We are now justified, when we find cross-cousin marriage in any other tribe, in concluding that here, too, it first fulfilled the function of alleviating tribute and later changed into a mechanism for enrichment.

Cross-cousin marriage can be inferred in its entirety from the marriage classes of the Kamilaori as described by Morgan in *Ancient Society*. After a great deal of effort, we were able to establish that the strange and complicated system of the Australian marriage classes is simply a manifestation of the universal institution of 'legal' cross-cousin marriage. Once this has been done, there is no longer any doubt – considering the fact that in everything else the organization of the Australians is quite similar to that of the Trobrianders – that the marriage gift also exists from clan to clan in some form or other. Otherwise, the whole complicated structure of marriage classes makes no sense.

First, let us repeat Morgan's description. The Kamilaori are divided into six clans, which, for marriage purposes are split into two sections:

I: (1) Goanna (Duli); (2) Kangaroo (Murriira);
    (3) Opossum (Mute)
II: (4) Emu (Dinoun); (5) Bandicoot (Bilba);
    (6) Blacksnake (Nurai)

Originally, the first three clans were not allowed to intermarry, because they were subdivisions of one original clan. In the beginning, then, there were only two clans. The later groups should not be called clans but rather phratries, on the model of the Greek groups. In addition to the division into two primeval clans, which we find split up into six daughter clans, there is a division into marriage classes. Each of the primeval clans consists of four marriage classes. There are eight in all, divided by sex – four male and four female:

MALE	FEMALE
1. Ippai	1. Ippata
2. Kumbo	2. Buta
3. Murri	3. Mata
4. Kubbi	4. Kapota

Each male and each female marriage class consists of the respective brothers and sisters, now separated. Consequently, Ippai and Ippata, Kumbo and Buta, Murri and Mata, Kubbi and Kapota are brothers and sisters and must not marry each other. But also, apart from this, they may not marry whom they will, which completely contradicts clan organization, according to which anyone from clan A would be allowed to marry anyone from clan B. Marriages are only permitted between:

> Ippai and Kapota
> Kumbo and Mata
> Murri and Buta
> Kubbi and Ippata

Thus, three quarters are excluded (a quarter of whom are brothers or sisters), and the choice can be made from among one fourth only. The system becomes even more complicated: whereas, since this is a matriliny, the children remain in the mother's clan, they pass, within this clan, to a different marriage class from their mother's, i.e.:

MALE	FEMALE		MALE	FEMALE
Ippai		Their		
marries	Kapota	children are	Murri and Mata
Kumbo		Their		
marries	Mata	children are	Kubbi and Kapota
Murri		Their		
marries	Buta	children are	Ippai and Ippata
Kubbi		Their		
marries	Ippata	children are	Kumbo and Buta

In following the parentage, we find that in the maternal line a Kapota is always the mother of a Mata and a Mata in turn the mother of a Kapota. Similarly, an Ippata is the mother of a Buta and a Buta in turn the mother of an Ippata. The same applies to the male classes.

The Kamilaori derive the two original clans from two primeval mothers. The connection of each child with a certain clan is also evident from the marriage law. Classes and primeval clans have the following relation:

Primeval clan I (Goanna, Kangaroo, Opossum), a primeval mother

Classes: Murri, Mata, Kubbi, and Kapota

Primeval clan II (Emu, Bandicoot, Blacksnake), a primeval mother

Classes: Kumbo, Buta, Ippai, and Ippata

Thus, the clan is preserved through the fact that it includes all the children of its female members. Morgan writes that very probably there were only two male and two female classes originally, which later were split into eight. We shall indicate our agreement with this thesis when we introduce our hypothesis of the origin of exogamy. But from the fact that the three sub-clans contain the same marriage classes, it follows that originally they were homogeneous clans. The subdivision into eight classes must have significance, as must the whole marriage order, which Morgan merely describes, giving no explanation. He only remarks that the class system is older than clan division, the second being a later development that chokes off the former. This explanation of Morgan's follows of necessity from his presupposition that the clans and the marriage taboo within the clan arose as the result of 'natural selection'. We can demonstrate that it was purely socioeconomic factors that led to the subdivision into marriage classes, just as other circumstances conditioned the division into four classes. The division into eight marriage classes, and therefore the further restriction of marriage to one fourth of the tribal members of the opposite sex, occurred to make possible the economically compensatory institution of cross-cousin marriage. We shall see that the practice it was to alleviate – the payment of tribute – resulted from the division into *four* classes.

If we examine parentage and marriage order closely, it becomes evident that *the sons of the brothers always marry the daughters of the sisters*. The daughters of the brothers never marry the sons of the sisters. There is no other possibility. *This, then, is a perfect system of cross-cousin marriage*, and it can have only one function, as it has with the Trobrianders –

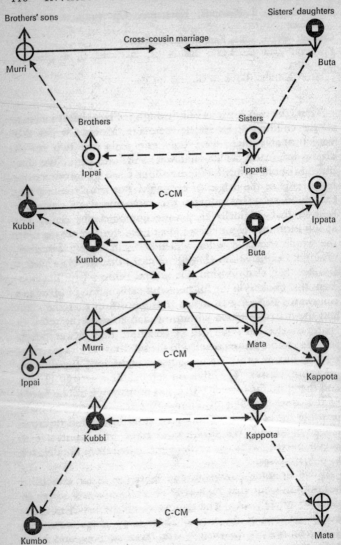

Figure 5. *The Australian marriage classes a a system of cross-cousin marriage*

the alleviation of tribute. First let us verify this statement by means of a table derived from Morgan's descriptions.

If we now look at the different classes, we see that a Buta woman is not just the daughter of an Ippata; she is also the niece (sister's daughter) of an Ippai and can marry only a Murri. The Murri would be the group-son of her mother's brother. We also see that a Murri belongs to one of the three sub-clans of primeval clan I, whereas his cousin, a Buta, belongs to primeval clan II, as do her mother and her mother's brother. Similarly an Ippata, who marries her cousin (mother's brother's son), a Kubi – together with her mother, a Buta, and her mother's brother, a Kumbo – all belong to the same primeval clan. The same applies to every Kapota and every Mata woman. Whatever marriage class we pick out and examine in its marriage relation to another, it is *always the brother's son who marries the sister's daughter.* In this class system any marriage other *than cross-cousin marriage is out of the question.* We shall discuss the economic implications in the following chapter.

Since the marriage gift has such a significant function, we are very interested in its origin. The period of loose marital bonds – that is, of pairing marriage – seems clearly to co-incide with the establishment of the institution of the marriage gift. But pairing marriage did not exist from the beginning, and the marriage gift must have developed from more primitive forms, from some sort of payment of tribute. But who paid this tribute and to whom? What could so deeply have affected the primal incestuous horde – in which paternity was not known because matings were unregulated and in particular because the role of the father was unknown (as it is unknown even today among the Trobrianders) – that it instituted a practice with such serious consequences? The payment of tribute, from clan to clan or from tribe to tribe, is found among the Trobrianders and among many other peoples. Within one clan, in a primevally work-democratic society, a tribute is senseless, whatever its form, and it does not occur. We find it, however, in the form of the *marriage gift from clan to clan in one tribe*, making one clan tributary to the

others, and eventually all the clans tributary to the chief'
family. What is the meaning of this? For the present we know
no more than that this economic institution is related to the
exogamy of the clans. To obtain a deeper insight, we mus
look into the origin of clan exogamy; in other words, the
incest taboo among the descendants of the same primeva
mother. We would not undertake such a study were it not fo
certain facts that at first sight seem unrelated but on close
observation appear to fit together.

6

The Origin of Clan Division and the Incest Taboo

RELICS OF PRIMEVAL TIMES

IT is recognized by most students of the primeval history of mankind that clan division and the incest taboo within the clan are central problems of primeval development. On this subject a number of more or less credible hypotheses have been proposed, among which Morgan's and Engels's, and Freud's, will engage our close attention later. They are generally characterized by the attempt to derive primeval conditions either from the supposed economic conditions of remote times or from the nature of human instinctual life. Freud was the first to recognize in the incest *taboos* the reaction to original incest *wishes*. From our *present* knowledge of the Trobrianders, thanks to Malinowski's accurate research, a hypothesis can be deduced that solves a series of problems without doing violence to the data. We would have refrained from proposing a new hypothesis had not some present-day institutions among the Trobrianders that seem relevant struck us as being relics of primeval times, making possible a reconstruction.

A hypothesis that is to explain plausibly the origin of the incest taboo must be sociobiological – i.e. it must show that the taboo arose of necessity out of the people's way of life; it must provide a solution to a number of problems; and it must not be at variance with the actual organization but must reproduce in the essentials its preliminary historical stage. The basic elements of the hypothesis, therefore, must be found in the present situation.

Our assumption can claim to be universally valid only if it provides a key to the problems discussed here, as well as to others.

We derive our hypothesis from the following facts about the Trobrianders:

1. The wife's brother is her actual supporter and the 'guardian' of her children. Only the genital relationship is lacking for him to be her husband. He belongs to the same clan as she does (this is so wherever there is clan organization).

2. He pays marriage tribute to the husband, who is a stranger and who has a genital relationship with the sister.

3. The husband belongs to a different clan and derives only advantage from the sexual bond with the sister of the supporting brother.

4. Trobriand society is divided into four clans, which are exogamous. The clans are of different rank; there are nobler and lesser clans.

5. Legend has it that the primeval mother emerged from a hole and gave birth to two children, a brother and a sister, who lived together in incest. The myth on the origin of the clans is as follows:

It is the rule in Trobriand mythology that, originally, only one couple emerged from each such 'hole,' a brother and a sister; she to start the lineage, he to protect her and look after her affairs. Thus the rule is: *one* clan, *one* village, *one* portion of garden-land, *one* system of gardening and fishing magic, *one* pair of brother and sister ancestors, *one* rank and *one* pedigree. (Malinowski, *The Sexual Life of Savages*, pp. 497–8)

Legend hands down a picture of a society springing from a brother-sister pair and organized in a primeval work-democracy, with incest. This group is later the clan. Now, the brother, who is even today the real husband of the sister except for the genital relationship, must enter into a relationship of economic obligation to her stranger-husband.

What brought about this double obligation, the renunciation of genitality with the sister and the tribute to her husband? Let us now fit in the first piece of our hypothesis – that the clans, contrary to general belief, did not originate from a division of primeval society through exogamy, but conversely, *that one clan, the originally self-contained primeval horde, imposed the incest taboo on the other clan, which was equally self-contained, or rather prohibited marriage within its own group.* Accordingly, *the clans,* later joined together, *were originally separate primeval hordes.* Why did one clan impose this prohibition on the other?

Let us further consider that the primeval hordes were not settled in one place but were nomadic hunters. Particularly after some natural catastrophe, the young men had to go off hunting and live in abstinence, wandering about for weeks, perhaps for months. When such a horde of hunting men came upon a stranger tribe living at peace, two things were bound to happen. The intruders would seize what the peaceful tribe had gathered, presumably killing a number of tribe members in the fighting; and they would steal the women, the men's sisters, in order to embrace them, to which they were especially incited by their abstinence. If they emerged victorious, it was easy to enslave the vanquished men, to prohibit them the genital embrace with their own sister-wives, and to bind them in some way to work for them.

In the course of hundreds and thousands of years, as man increased in number and migrations became more frequent, such catastrophes were bound to recur more and more often, so that the stealing of women and the imposition of tribute on their brother-husbands became a *custom.* In these clashes between primeval hordes the advantage could not remain with the victors. The vanquished would take revenge on their attackers when they had retreated (later, clan vendettas), or the victorious horde might be attacked by a third horde, with similar consequences. These incidents must have brought such uncertainty to the originally peaceful organization of the primeval hordes that mutual fear led to their alliance into tribes, retaining matriliny (the clan division of the tribes) and giving a peaceful sanction to what had earlier been forced – i.e. to *the introduction of reciprocal marriage between two primeval hordes. The original prohibition from outside, by the victors, of the sexual embrace within one's own clan became, in the course of time, the established custom in the clan.* But the earlier arrangement, that the male relatives of the women, i.e. their once brother-husbands, provide for their economic needs, was retained, all the more so as it brought advantages to the victorious clan.

With the alliance of the hordes (clans) into tribes and with the introduction of reciprocal marriage (exogamy) and the continuation of the manner of providing for the women within the framework of *their own* clan, peace and quiet could return to the organization. As the economic provision rested on reciprocity, no other consequences would have been forthcoming had not one clan inevitably been the original victor and the other the vanquished. Under the circumstances, the victorious clan would have to maintain its position in some way. It was justified in considering itself 'superior' and in deriving certain economic advantages from this. It could, for example, determine that its elder would become 'chief' or military leader of both clans (tribal chief) and enjoy certain privileges, such as receiving additional marriage gifts or tribute. Thus, the chief's claim to polygamy need not have existed from the beginning. On the contrary, it could be a result of his economic ascendancy, which automatically arose from the greater quantity of marriage gifts received by him. Thus, the institution of a chieftainship and the division of the clans according to rank can easily be derived from the relationship of victor to vanquished.

Let us summarize:

1. Two primeval hordes, living peacefully at some distance from each other, organized according to natural law, in a primeval work-democracy, and in incest.

2. Economic or natural reasons (change of hunting grounds) cause them to come into conflict.

3. The men of one primeval horde, while wandering and, of necessity, living in abstinence, attack the other, resulting in the prohibition of the genital embrace in the clan attacked (*external*, ultimately *economic*, *origin of incest taboo*) and imposition of tribute on the former brother-husbands.

4. Retaliation by the brothers, mutual destruction, *primeval catastrophe*, introducing violence in hitherto peaceful

primeval society and mutual fear between the men of the hostile hordes.

5. Re-establishment of peace through alliance and regularization of status quo 'by contract' – i.e. *institution of reciprocal marriage* (*exogamy*), with maintenance of the economic advantages resulting from the lasting sexual unions (later marriage institution).

6. A token of the victory of the one clan over the other is retained in that the clans are of *different rank* and have a *common chief*. This becomes the primary impulse in the development from natural right through mother-right to father-right.[26]

Among the Trobrianders, we see the primeval hordes peacefully united in tribes but split into exogamous clans. There is payment of tribute by the brothers to the husbands; polygamy of the chief, as a late result of his original ascendancy; and primary matriliny side by side with incipient father-right. We have already seen how class division and negative sexual morality derive from these conditions.

Let us now test the validity of our hypothesis against further data and evidence taken from other peoples, before discussing objections and analysing the Morgan–Engels and Freud hypotheses of the origin of the incest taboo.

We have assumed that the endogamous tribes of primeval peoples, which consist of clans or gentes, in America as well as in Europe, in Australia as well as in India and Africa, did not originate through division from within but through the union of alien, *originally hostile primeval hordes, which constitute the later clans*. We inferred this from present-day conditions among the Trobrianders and derived the rest from it.

1. Morgan and Engels concluded from the stone implements of the earlier Stone Age, which excavations have uncovered in all continents, that in the savage period of mankind, when fishing began and fire was discovered, migrations were universal. Morgan postulated the pure consanguine family living in incest. Hunting and cannibalism characterize this

26. Natural right could be said to correspond to the primeval incestuous situation; mother-right, to exogamous clan organization.

stage, which is that of a great many Australian and Poly-nesian peoples today. But that is not as significant as Morgan's statement that the clan consists of a solid circle of kin in the female line, distinguished from other clans of the same tribe by common institutions of its own of a social and religious nature. Engels, working from his concept of the splintering of the original clans into a tribal organization, assumed that it was a case of 'consolidation' through special customs of the clans. Is it not more probable that the fact that the clans differ in their mythology, as well as in other respects, is rather an indication of their *original* self-contained nature and not of a *later* consolidation of groupings within the tribe? Wherever there are clans, we see this clan unity in all their functions (matrilineal inheritance, common descent, common grounds, clan solidarity, etc.) which distinguish them as a group from the other clans of the same tribe. Among the Trobrianders the separate origin of each clan is as obvious as among the Iroquois, the Romans, etc.

2. Morgan found eight clans among the Iroquois, each tracing itself back to a different animal. Thus, the tribe could not have originated through a division into clans, but only as the result of an alliance of clans.

3. We see the process of fusion in human organizational groups among the American Indians as well as among the Romans. The legend of the 'founding of Rome,' writes Engels, 'shows that the first settlement was effected by a number of *Latin clans united into a tribe* (a hundred, according to legend), which were soon joined by a Sabellian tribe that is said to have numbered a hundred clans too, and finally by a third' [Italics, Reich]. Engels himself mentions (p. 119) that 'here little of the original organization was left except for the clan. The foreheads of many members of the tribe indicate blood mix-ture, mostly with other Indians, conforming to the image of the original authentic tribe.' Engels seeks here to uphold the division hypothesis, which is intended to support Morgan's concept of the origin of exogamy in natural selection. We see, however, that at the time of Morgan's observations the Iroquois, already constituted into tribes, behave in the same

way we assumed the primeval clan hordes behaved – i.e. *there is peace within the tribe and hostility outside it; enemy tribes fight and then make peace*, joining together in larger entities, with tribute being imposed. That is at variance with the division theory, which is not supported by present-day data and which rests on the assumption that the increase in the population and 'natural selection' through the exclusion of kin necessitated the internal division through exogamy. Elsewhere, Morgan says that, among various American Indian tribes with more than five or six clans, three or four are found joined together in a special group, 'fraternity', or phratry – a fact that Engels also mentions in his studies. Here, too, there is alliance, not division.

Moreover, the exact description Morgan gives of clan organization upholds the primary nature of the clan: election of the Sachem (administrator in peacetime) and of the chief (military leader); ban on the election of the chief's son, who is of a different clan, in favour of the sister's son; right of inheritance within the clan; an obligation of mutual protection; vendetta by the whole clan if one of their members is slain by someone from another clan (thus the clans become hostile to one another); the existence of clan names that only the clan may use; individual religious customs. Among the Seneca the tradition was that 'Bear' and 'Stag' were the two original clans from which the others branched off.

In Morgan, too, we learn that the names of the tribes seemingly originated by accident instead of having been chosen deliberately. Tribes were often given their names by other tribes; the name 'Teutons', for example, was bestowed upon the Germans by the Celts.

We must leave it to later investigations to ascertain to what extent the theory of internal division and that of an original union of primeval clans are justified. Among the Trobrianders, for instance, we see the tribe split into unrelated clans. The clans, however, are divided into distantly consanguineous sub-clans.

4. Among the Greeks, one finds nobler and lesser clans, just as among the Trobrianders. This is easily explained

by our derivation of the division by rank from the relationship between victor and vanquished clans. But we fail to understand how a clan consisting of members with equal rights could be split into subdivisions of different rank. In the second case, the later tribe would have had to be the original clan, which conflicts with the concept of one overall organization.

5. Apart from the brothers' obligation to pay tribute to their sisters' husbands, the strongest evidence that the clans were originally alien to each other is found in the strange courtship customs not only of the Trobrianders (the *ulatile* and the *katuyausi* expeditions) but of other tribes.

Consider the following description of a custom among the Samoans:

From personal observation Kubary gives a graphic description of a *Samoan youth's* courtship of the girl he has chosen and of her love. In Samoa, so quiet in the day time, the young people of both sexes gather in the Malae in the evening. A young warrior of well-groomed appearance stands near a group of young girls ... He stands erect and gesticulates with his raised arms in such a way that the whole of his head shakes. *He stamps his foot, he paces backwards, he stretches his arm forward as though he was armed with a spear, then he swings it round in a circle as if he was about to smash his enemy with a club. Undoubtedly he is a warrior telling his beautiful listeners about his feats, his victories.* They are all eyes and ears. One can see how strong an impression his account makes on the young girls, who cheer him enthusiastically. Then he asks some comrades to join him in a song ... Our narrator is the first to sing, all those present form the choir; yet the singing does not last very long ... The warrior stands up and steps in front of one of the most beautiful maidens. *She hesitates; almost unwillingly she allows herself to be pushed near by her friends* and to be drawn out into the open by the handsome dancer ...

A sugar-cane field is a safe hiding place for two lovers at night. Nobody will disturb them here in the hour of ghosts and spectres. Our couple know that and one can hear them speak without fear of being overheard. 'You know, *Lilomajava*, that my parents hate you, only the *awanga* is left us.' The *awanga*, the flight, is arranged and is to take place on the third night ... On the beach of the neighbouring village there is silence but on the white sands dark figures move. A *toumalua*, the native travelling canoe, is pushed into the water. The dark figures have disappeared, an upright triangular sail unfolds and glides along the beach, it disappears from sight. Only after it has gone a great distance is the muffled sound of a triton horn heard. This sound accompanies the happy couple along the coast announcing something special to the inhabitants, who are roused from their sleep. It hurries ahead of them to *Palauli* where the lovers will stay till their parents' anger has cooled . . .

The next morning there is commotion in both villages. The happy bridegroom's friends walk through their village shouting: '*Awanga!! Awanga!!* The beautiful *Tanetasi* and the brave *Lilo-majava* are *awanga!! awanga!!*' The bride's proud parents hear with suppressed anger the public proclamation which seals their daughter's destiny. For some time angry feelings prevail everywhere. The old fathers avoid each other, the young men look at their clubs and spears, but the main role is played by the young couple . . . After a few weeks everything calms down and the parents send their daughter a white mat as a sign of forgiveness. The couple who up to now have kept at a distance from each other return. The *feiainga* is carried out and the white mat with traces of the bride's worth upon it is exchanged for part of the dowry. The other part is handed over on the first confinement . . . If the pair do not marry out of love or if there are no difficulties to be expected, everything is arranged by the relatives. In former times the *awanga* (flight of the bride) was the order of the day in Samoa.[27]

The poetic mood of the writer cannot blind us to the fact that the courtship does not reflect a serious present-day situation. Various parts are played by various people. The villages stand in playful hostility towards each other. If these were not historic customs but actual acts of violence, if the parents were really angry, matters would turn out differently. But, as it is, everything runs its peaceful course. In earlier times the flight of the bride was an everyday occurrence – in primeval times as a real abduction (the suitor in the guise of a fierce warrior); later as a custom that gradually dies

27. Ploss-Bartels, 'Brautwerbung und Brautstand', 'Das Weib in der Natur–und Menschenkunde', *Geschlecht und Gesellschaft*, vol. 12, p. 548.

out, even as a recurring dream that reflects an actual traumatic situation eventually fades away.

Let us now add Malinowski's account of the *ulatile* expedition of the Trobriand young men. Echoes of the primeval abduction of women can definitely be heard:

There are two forms of *ulatile* expeditions to which the word applies in a somewhat technical sense. The first is a matter of necessity: a lover must visit his sweetheart in her own village. If, on one of the several occasions described in the previous section, two people from different communities have become strongly attracted by each other, they will arrange a meeting. As a rule the boy has some intimate friend in the girl's village, and this makes things easier, since this friend will help him. It is a matter of etiquette for the lover to adorn himself for the tryst, and this compels him to observe a certain measure of secrecy. He will not walk on the main road, but surreptitiously steal through the bush. 'Like a sorcerer he will go; stop and listen; go sideways and push through the jungle; no one must see him.' Thus one of my informants likened such *ulatile* to the clandestine expeditions of sorcerers [28] who, on their nocturnal expeditions, must not be seen by anybody.

As he approaches the village he has to be specially careful. In his own village such a passing intrigue, if discovered, would only arouse the jealousy of the accredited lover and start a minor quarrel. But an erotic poacher caught in another community might be seriously mishandled, not only by the jealous lover, but by all the other boys. He might also bring upon his sweetheart the reproaches of her regular lover. *However, the main reason for secrecy is that it is enjoined by custom as a rule of the game.* The two usually arrange to meet in the jungle near the girl's village. Sometimes the girl guides her lover to the chosen place by lighting a fire; sometimes they agree to imitate the call of a bird; sometimes she marks the way into the chosen spot of the jungle by tearing the leaves in a pattern or by placing leaves on the road.

28. In the evil spirits and sorcerers who play such a considerable part in the emotional life and mythology of primitive peoples, it is not difficult to recognize the powerful foreign invader. In the imagination of human beings who had never seen a stranger, had never even thought of the possibility that they existed, they were bound to appear as supernatural beings. Similarly, when America was discovered, the whites were at first worshipped by the natives, until their quite earthly nature was revealed.

. . . Sometimes a group of boys, who have brought away specially pleasant memories of another community from some festive gathering, will decide to go there in a body, on a regular *ulatile* expedition. Here secrecy is necessary, too. For though such expeditions are *customary and, in a way, lawful*, they constitute an encroachment on the rights of two other groups, the ordinary sweethearts of the *ulatile* boys, and the youths of the other village. If caught by either party the adventurers would have to face a volley of abuse, or even of blows; for girls in the Trobriands can defend their rights by force, and the boys in each community regard their women-folk as their own preserve. The adventurers would, therefore, usually steal out at night and put on their ornaments outside their village. But once on the main road, they become boisterous and defiant, for this is the proper behaviour on such an occasion. There are even some special bawdy songs, called *lo uwa*, to which they keep time as they go along. (*Sexual Life of Savages*, pp. 263–5; Reich's italics)

An example of such a song is:

'Hoho! I awake from my sleep, I hear the festive beat of the drums, as they throb with dance music – attracting women with full-dress skirts, with festive skirts on their flanks. With his song on his mouth, with his small drum in his hand, his teeth blackened, Tokivina rhythmically treads in the village of Wavivi, he walks in dancing rhythm through the village of Wavivi. (pp. 266–7)

Such songs . . . were also sung in olden days to indicate that the party was neither on the warpath nor on a sorcery expedition, nor bent on any other real mischief. As they approach their goal they become quiet again, for they must not be seen by the village youths. The girls, of course, know when the expedition is drawing near, for everything has been previously arranged in detail. The visitor most familiar with the village creeps near, and gives the agreed signal. One by one the girls sneak out of the houses and meet their lovers in the bush. Sometimes the girls are already awaiting them at some pre-arranged meeting place outside. Should this gathering of lovers be detected, a fight might ensue, leading, in former times, even to war between the two communities. (p. 267)

Certain contradictions are apparent here. On the one hand, such 'love expeditions' are a custom; in a certain sense, even 'a legitimate right'. On the other hand, serious fighting sometimes ensues between the members of the *ulatile* expedition and the local youths. These contradictions can be understood, however, if we think back to the fundamental institutions of the Trobrianders. For then the *ulatile* expedition is seen as a relic from primeval times when the men of one primeval clan invaded another clan.

We find here an instance of natural jealousy side by side with full social support of the institution of the love expedition. The clandestine behaviour, too, seems more a custom deriving from the abductions of primeval times than something arising out of actual circumstances.

Here let us quote Malinowski's account of a strange custom that still exists on the southern Trobriand Islands:

Now this communal weeding when practised by women of the villages of Okayaulo, Bwage, Kumilabwaga, Louya, Bwadela, or by the villages of Vakuta, gives weeders a curious privilege. If they perceive a stranger, a man from any village but their own, passing within sight, they have the customary right to attack him, a right which by all accounts they exercise with zeal and energy.

The man is the fair game of the women for all that sexual violence, obscene cruelty, filthy pollution, and rough handling can do to him. Thus first they pull off and tear up his pubic leaf, the protection of his modesty and, to a native, the symbol of his manly dignity. Then, by masturbatory practices and exhibitionism, they try to produce an erection in their victim and, when their manoeuvres have brought about the desired result, one of them squats over him and inserts his penis into her vagina. After the first ejaculation he may be treated in the same manner by another woman. Worse things are to follow. Some of the women will defecate and micturate all over his body, paying special attention to his face, which they pollute as thoroughly as they can. 'A man will vomit, and vomit, and vomit,' said a sympathetic informant. Sometimes these furies rub their genitals against his nose and mouth, and use his fingers and toes, in fact any projecting part of his body, for lascivious purposes. The natives from the north are very much amused by this custom, which they despise or affect to despise. They love to enter into details, and to demonstrate by convincing mimicry. Local informants from the south confirmed this account in all essentials. They were by no means ashamed of their custom, regarding it rather as a sign of the general virility of the district, and passing on any possible opprobrium to the stranger-victims.

Some of my local informants added that at the *yausa*, as this custom is called, women would throw off their fibre skirts, and naked 'like a band of *tauva'u*' (evil spirits) pounce upon the man. He also added that hair would be torn from the man's head, and that he would be lacerated and beaten till he was too weak to get up and move away.

... At the same time, I had a practical demonstration of the contrast between the way in which such a custom is represented by those who have it, and by those who do not. By the local men it was obviously caricatured as a shameful and savage habit. But the southern visitors, some of whom had come from Okayaulo and Bwadela, the home of the *yausa*, took, in a later conversation, a different view, showing no embarrassment whatever. They told me boastfully that no stranger ever dared to enter their district at that time, that they themselves were the only people free to walk about, that their women were the best garden-weeders and the most powerful people in the island. (pp. 274–5, 278–9)

This custom strikes one as a relic from primeval times, when women learned to defend themselves against intruders from foreign tribes. The manner of their revenge reflects their actual experience; they anticipate what they are afraid the man might do to them: they violate him. *Peace within, violence without* – that was the primeval situation. Alliance of the hostile hordes into one peaceful tribe divided into clans was the solution; it meant a return to tranquillity. But traces of violence remained in the subdivision of the clans according to rank and in the marriage tribute. These, in turn, led to more violence.[29]

Let us hasten to mention some other peoples among whom are found the typical customs of the marriage gift, joint meals as a symbol of economic alliance when the marriage is contracted, and the ceremonial abduction of women. The fact that in all the studies we see reference to one or another detail from the complex of rites found in full force among the

29. In his book *Die Psychoanalyse primitiver Kulturen*, Roheim describes the distribution rite among the Papuas in the Luai District. It not only agrees in essence with the rite described by Malinowski but supplements our knowledge of the psychic conflicts accompanying the payment of the marriage tribute.

Trobrianders encourages us to assume that most of the peoples of the globe probably underwent the same process of fighting hostile hordes, followed by subsequent peaceful alliance. The omnipresence of the incest taboo and of the marriage institution thereby loses much of its enigmatic character.

Max Ebert in his *Reallexikon der Vorgeschichte* gives a compilation of ethnological facts from which we take the following:

Throughout all of South-West Asia it is the custom that the couple eat a common meal from one dish when the marriage is contracted. (Quoted from Skeat and Blagden, in Ebert's *Reallexikon*)

Legends among the Tschuktschen tell of the 'abduction' of girls by men of other tribes, by ghosts, eagles, whales, ravens, etc. But it also happened in former times that a few young people would get together and abduct a young girl, tie her hands and feet, and take her to the house of a man who wanted her for his wife. Not only the men of stranger families but even relatives and cousins often did this when they had been refused by the father or by the girl. After such an abduction, the parents usually received another woman from the abductor's family in exchange for their daughter. Marriages by flight, in cases where the parents refuse their consent, occur very seldom. (Czaplicka, pp. 72 ff.)

Similarly, among the Camchadales, the woman must be earned by the man. When he has been given permission to take his bride, a ceremony takes place in which he has to take possession of her by force. All the women of the village try to protect her from him. In addition, she is dressed in several heavy garments which are bound tightly around her so that she looks like a stuffed figure. The ceremony now consists in his having to tear her clothes from her body and then to touch her genitals with his hands. Meanwhile the other women try to defend her. (Ebert, p. 251)

On the Andaman Isles, among the hunting tribes, marriages are arranged by the elder men and women.

... Sometimes the parents promise their small children ... Also the parents take upon themselves all other arrangements for the marriage of their children. The parents of the young man do not, however, themselves talk to a girl's family but ask one or several of their friends to act as mediators ... From the moment the possibility of a union is considered, the man's parents avoid talking to the girl's and any message between them is transmitted by a third person. In this way they also send each other food and other objects. The recipient of such a gift always hastens to hand over a counter gift of equal value. If the marriage takes place, the parents of both partners enter into a special relationship entailing certain duties. From the beginning of maturity to the time when they marry, the young men on the Andaman Isles live in a bachelors' house. (Brown, quoted in Ebert, p. 253)

The Koita and Motus tribes of southern New Guinea have the same premarital customs as the Trobrianders, the same courtship and wedding customs ... Gifts are handed over for years by both families, particularly food gifts. (Seligman, pp. 76 ff., 253)

Among the Tillamook on the coast of Oregon in North-West America ... his relatives collected food of all sorts and even made money contributions for the purchase of the girl. The girl's relatives promised certain gifts for her ... After the marriage celebration the people were treated to berries, fish and meat and then the bride's father distributed more food among the young man's relatives which they took home with them. (p. 255)

Among the Chukmas of South-East India both the bridegroom and the bride must behave timidly at the wedding ceremony of the common meal. (Lewin, quoted in Ebert, p. 258.) [We are reminded of the shyness of the newly married among the Trobrianders.]

To this day the connection between the Wahhabi tribes of the Njed, the mountain plateau of the interior of Arabia, is only maintained by marriages which are contracted between first cousins. (S. A. Powell, *World's Work*, 1923)

Among the Nalit Eskimos of the Bering Strait marriages between first cousins frequently take place with the idea that in times of scarcity the woman is nearer to the man. In the case of want, they say, the woman would otherwise steal from the man and the man would starve. But as it is she looks after him. (Nelson, *The Eskimos about Bering Strait*, 1899)

THE MORGAN–ENGELS HYPOTHESIS OF EXOGAMY

To explain the prohibition of marriage within the clan, Morgan, and after him Engels, assumed that the law of exogamy or the incest taboo was a product of the 'principle of natural

selection'. The forbidding of marriage between even col-
lateral kinsmen constitutes, according to Morgan, 'an excellent
illustration of how the principle of natural selection takes
effect.' Engels adds:

It is beyond doubt that these tribes in which incest was restricted by this progressive step of necessity developed more
quickly and more fully than those in which marriage between
brothers and sisters remained the rule. And how deeply the effect
of this progress was felt is proved by the institution of the clan
which directly sprang from it and which forms the basis of the
social order of most, if not all the barbaric peoples of the world.
(*The Origin of the Family*)

And when discussing the division of the Kamilaori into
marriage classes, according to which maternal cousins of the
first degree cannot be husband and wife – only those of the
second degree can – Engels remarks: 'One sees, the urge to
prevent incest again asserts itself, but quite gropingly in a
naturally primitive way, without clear consciousness of the
goal' (p. 28).

Thus, both Morgan and Engels attributed the division of
the tribe into gentes to the splitting up of an originally consanguineous tribe. Both had been influenced by the recently
propounded Darwinian theory of natural selection, which
they extended to the elimination of incest. This view can no
longer be maintained, for the following reasons:

1. Incest has never been proved harmful. Early Soviet
sexual legislation was right, therefore, in adopting the view
that the incest law is senseless, when incest is harmless. The
only possible connection between natural selection and incest
is that morbid dispositions accumulate if brother *and* sister
are both *ill*. But the situation is exactly the same when two
persons who are not related by blood procreate if they both
have a morbid disposition. Moreover, as medical research
increasingly restricts the effects of heredity, turning instead
to the social causes of widespread diseases such as tuber-
culosis, that principle proportionately loses its validity.

2. Morgan's and Engels's assumption presupposes that

primitive man knew the role of the father in procreation and was able to assess the supposed harm to the offspring of an incestuous union and to make the connection between the two. The first cannot have been the case, and Morgan himself is elsewhere of the opinion, confirmed by Malinowski's research, that with the then unregulated state of genital life, paternity *must* have been unknown. Moreover, we are justified in assuming that man at the stage of savagery lived in incest for thousands of years without being in the least harmed by it. There is no proof that greater advances were made after the introduction of exogamy, and even if this were the case, an explanation may be found in the advantageous effects of the mixing of different tribes, after peace was made, which may have stimulated technical or cultural progress.

3. The most important objection to the thesis that exogamy originated in the principle of natural selection is the fact that even if the primeval tribes had divided into clans, they could not have done away with kinship. No matter how far a tribe might have branched out through its children and its children's children, they all came from blood-related primeval pairs of brothers and sisters. This was overlooked by Morgan and Engels. Thus it follows that, to uphold the very hypothesis of natural selection, one has to assume the mingling of two *not consanguineous* – that is, entirely foreign – primeval clans. Accordingly, the clan must have existed before the tribe, which adds fresh support to our concept of the joining together of clans into tribes.

Thus we have explained the origin of the incest taboo and its further development on *biosociological* grounds instead of through natural selection. The riddle of the Kamilaori's complicated division into marriage classes, first into four, then into eight – which Morgan attributed to natural selection, and which he thought offered an explanation of the punalua practice – lends itself to a sociological solution, as follows:

Originally, there were four marriage classes, two male and two female, which could marry only crosswise. Later, through a further division, eight classes came into being. We regard the

last division as an offshoot of the widespread introduction o
cross-cousin marriage, which was meant to *compensate* for th
payment of tribute, as it does among the Trobrianders. Th
payment of tribute, therefore, cannot have existed always
Not only must it have been related to a particular system o
marriage, but it must have caused this system to come int
being. The division into four classes followed as a matter o
course from the division of two primeval clans each into a
women's class (sisters' class) and a men's class (brother'
class), which, after the conclusion of peace and the alliance o
the clans, entered into crosswise marriage (mutual exogamy)
The punalua family was thus the first stage in the family *afte*
the alliance, just as the consanguine family was the last ste
before the encounter of the two clans. The brothers had to pay
marriage tribute to the husbands, or at any rate make gifts
linked to the marriage. The victorious tribe, according to ou
hypothesis, had secured advantages for itself: for instance
payment of special tribute to the chief or military leader
who among the Trobrianders is from the 'noblest' clan. Tha
meant a one-sided burden for the defeated clan. From this
must have arisen the need for relief such as only cross-cousin
marriage could provide. And out of this need came the furthe
division into *eight* classes, which represents the perfect system
of compensatory matings. The rest is unclear. But we saw
among the Trobrianders that the chief's ascendancy was not
eliminated. Perhaps that was why he sought a partial compensation for the loss the division into eight classes entailed
for him. The confirmation or refutation of this theory must be
left to later research.

THE FREUDIAN HYPOTHESIS OF THE MURDER OF THE PRIMEVAL FATHER

Freud bases his reconstruction of primeval history on Dar-
win's theory that among the apes there are families, which
live alone and in which the chief male does not tolerate any
other males. The 'primeval father', who is envisioned on
the model of this chief ape, in Freud's concept, would always

chase away his adult sons. At some point the brothers conspired together, slew the father, ate him, and thus put an end to the primeval father's horde. Here Freud utilized Atkinson's observation that the lead stallions in a herd of horses often clashed with other roaming stallions. He cites Atkinson's theory according to which the horde disintegrates because of the ensuing quarrel of the sons, which prevents the development of a new organization. On the other hand, Freud believes that it is precisely in the killing of the primeval father that 'social organization, moral restrictions and religion' (*Totem and Taboo*) originate. To give credence to this sequence of events – the origin of religion and of the social order in the murder of the primeval father – Freud argues that one need only 'assume that the conspiring group of brothers was dominated by the same contradictory feelings towards their father as we find in the ambivalence of the father complex in all our children and neurotics. They hated the father, who stood so much in the way of their need for power and their sexual claims, but they also loved and admired him. After they had done away with him, satisfied their hatred and carried out their wish for identification with him, the tender feelings which had been suppressed in the process could be expressed again. This took the form of repentance ... What the father had formerly prevented by his existence they themselves now prohibited in the psychic situation of subsequent obedience which is so well-known to us from psychoanalysis ... They refuted their action by forbidding the killing of the father-substitute, the totem, and renounced its fruits by denying themselves the women who had been set free. Thus, out of their filial guilt feelings they created the two fundamental taboos of totemism,' the *prohibition of incest* and of the killing of the totem animal. The totem animal, consequently, was thought by Freud to be the 'natural and nearest substitute for the father'.

A series of arguments by Freud, and particularly the whole psychoanalytic ethnology, developed subsequently by Roheim, Reik, and others of his students, are based on this hypothesis of the murder of the primeval father. Since the views that we have evolved here contradict this premise, it is necessary to go into its basic elements in greater detail.

It seems to provide a compact interpretation of primeval development, and at first it is satisfying because it applies to primeval times well-known clinical findings from analytical practice which have been tested hundreds of times. It also explains, with apparent effortlessness, the two key problems, totemism and the origin of the incest taboo. In spite of this, however, some of its suppositions do not correspond to the facts.

1. The first supposition is that the primeval horde consisted of one strong male adult, the father of the group; several women, his wives and daughters; and several sons. If the primeval father, supposing he did exist, again and again chased away the sons when they matured – and that cannot have happened once only and in only one place but must have happened often and all over the world, throughout the millennia – it is incomprehensible how any primeval horde managed to propagate itself, withstand the struggle with nature, and establish a culture. Furthermore, when did the expulsions take place? Among primitive peoples genital life begins at a very early age, long before puberty. Were male children expelled as soon as they had coitus? This *cannot* be correct.

If, as in Roheim, reference is made to legends of a father killed in primeval times, one must remember that the father group consisted originally of *strangers* – this is obvious from clan division – with whom the members of the son group were in conflict, not because of the son relationship but because of earlier hostilities between alien hordes. That has nothing to do with incest. The Oedipus complex could arise only *after* the hordes joined together, *after* close-knit families were formed.

2. Another supposition is that the sons denied themselves the genital embrace with their mothers and sisters; consequently, these women were without husbands, and the sons were, as before, without wives. Why did the group not die out, then? The contention that the men took women from

other groups leads to nebulous speculations, considering how thinly populated the world was in the earliest days of human history. Here, too, we go astray.

3. To uphold the hypothesis, it is also necessary to postulate the *natural* violent jealousy of the males and the biological ambivalence of feelings. But the assumption of the jealousy of savages as proposed by Freud becomes questionable in the face of the following facts. First, consider the sexual ceremonies of primitive peoples, and especially the sexual life of the Trobrianders, as described by Malinowski; jealousy is excluded. Consider also the fact that violent jealousy, as we know it in our society, came into being with the marriage bond, when economic interests turned natural jealousy into a vehement claim to property; and, finally, the fact that monogamous marriage is a late manifestation in human society. As to ambivalence of feelings, we must first determine to what extent this is a result of social conditions (restriction of genital gratification; hence, the emergence of an attitude of hatred towards a denying world: ambivalence). Psychoanalytic experience with psychically sick people unequivocally shows that ambivalence *may* indeed exist as a tendency in the instinctual apparatus, but what we see in the sick person *has developed through the restriction of his genital needs*, and that is non-existent in primeval society. Essentially, then, ambivalence is *socially* conditioned. Its form and intensity depend upon the manner in which libidinous needs are satisfied; therefore, being a social consequence, it cannot be the primeval basis of human culture. We have also seen in the mourning rites of the Trobrianders how a specific historical relationship of production creates ambivalence of feeling. If the wife's relatives did not stand in a relationship of tribute to the husband, they would have no reason to be ambivalent and to hide their hatred in rigorous mourning rites. And if ambivalence dominates the inner life of twentieth-century man, one must ask what its social causes are. Such ambivalence cannot simply be ascribed to primitive man who matures and lives under altogether different conditions. We can be certain that the Trobriand child does not develop any wrong notions

of sex, since he knows that, except for the incest wish, he
need not repress genitality, but is allowed to gratify it. No
fixations of penis envy or masculinity complexes develop in
little girls, because the social atmosphere does not accord the
boy a privileged position, as it does with us. That comes in
with patriarchal authority and inheritance along the father's
line. Thus, we do not deny the analytical findings. However,
not considering them biologic but historical, we try to place
them in the right connection to the history of society.

4. The other hypothesis, that the sons denied themselves
the practice of incest out of guilt feelings, stems from the
assumption of the *natural* ambivalence of feelings. It is
supposed to be the origin of morality. That is a *petitio principii.*
For what must first be explained is here presupposed. Guilt
feelings are themselves the expression of a moral reaction;
therefore, they cannot explain the origin of morality.

Freud regards the religious concept of the fall of man,
from which Jesus would redeem mankind, as the expression of
a primeval act of murder. The biblical myth of Adam and
Eve, however, as well as the whole Catholic ideology of
original sin, reveals itself essentially as the myth of a sexual
crime, as the concept of sinning against a sexual restriction.
That does not exclude the possibility that this sexual crime was
accompanied by an act of murder. Our derivation of the
incest taboo *implicitly* contains the historical primeval murder,
when two alien hordes clashed. In those circumstances, the
first moral precepts doubtless originated from sexual prohibitions that have nothing to do with the Oedipus complex –
for the Oedipus complex is historically younger than sexual
suppression. And, as we have said, the later father-group was,
originally, a horde of strangers. So the concept of the murder
of the primeval father corresponds to a combination of two
things that are far apart in time: a bloody clash with men who
were not the fathers but from whose clan sprang the *later* real
fathers who were *not* murdered.

5. The Freudian hypothesis does not allow the possibility
that incest existed in primeval times. It has, however, been
proved from myths and from direct observation that incest

was prevalent for thousands of years. Also, the ignorance of fatherhood, which is obvious from the sexual life of primeval societies, contradicts the core of the Freudian interpretation.[30]

6. The Freudian concept cannot be reconciled with the typical legends of the origin of clans from two or several primeval mothers or primeval brother–sister pairs. It is based on the assumption of son–mother incest, but in reality it was brother–sister incest that was decisive. The confirmation of the existence of a primeval father, which Roheim sought to provide, is based on the existence of a totem animal. But first it must be proved that the totem animal did *in the beginning* represent the primeval father. Neither the interpretation of the incestuously desired sister as a mother-substitute nor the interpretation of the totem as an original father-substitute is conclusive without historical derivation.

7. According to Freud, the incest taboo must be thought of as operative within the family. The incest taboo, however, dominates the *whole* clan. As the family was a much later development, the restriction of the incest taboo to members of the family – father, mother, children – is a late result and therefore irrelevant to primeval history.

To sum up: the Freudian hypothesis is at variance with fundamental institutions of primitive organization (*two* incestuous primeval clans, incest taboo within the clan, promiscuity and incest in the primeval stage, an original organization along the maternal line, etc.) and it so seriously neglects the historical development of the family in relation

30. One could object with some justification that ignorance of fatherhood is convincing during the stage of promiscuity but not when monogamous pairing marriage evolves. In addition, it would not be difficult to conclude from the Trobrianders' attitude towards fatherhood that they repress their knowledge of the role of the father. The assumption of such a repression does not preclude ignorance during the promiscuous stage. It is conceivable that affective denial of the clan-alien men after the union of the hordes was so intense that their fatherhood was not acknowledged – but that requires further research. Another consideration is the fact that acknowledgement of fatherhood would have severely shaken the matriarchal system of clan kinship.

to the socioeconomic development that it is difficult to uphold.

Thus far, we have explained the proscription against eating the totem animal and against living in incest as having originated in a historical event: the victorious clan prohibited the defeated clan from hunting and eating the animal prevalent in the particular hunting area and from having genital embrace with the women of their own clan. These prohibitions did not originate within the clan but were imposed from outside by a victorious group. In certain festivities of primitive peoples in which there is promiscuous intercourse and eating of the totem animal, we recognize the sanctioning of a breakthrough of the old rules between hordes, the expression of a longing for the more peaceful organization of the incestuous horde, which knows no obligation other than to provide for its own clan. It is, above all, the barriers of primitive pairing-marriage, and occasionally also of the incest taboo – relatively late developments of human society – that fall during these festivities. Freud's premise that these totem-meal festivals represent the murder of the primeval father is, even from his own point of view, at variance with the breaking down of the incest barrier on these occasions. Do men perhaps allow themselves, at a much higher stage of organization, what they denied themselves at a stage of cultureless savagery? Had they at that time, as savages, stronger guilt feelings than today? And, if so, why?

Conceivably, further research will link the legends of the murder of the primeval father and the clashes of primeval hordes. The totem animal *secondarily* became a symbol for the primeval mother and later, in the patriarchal organization, a symbol for the patriarch. We are of the opinion, therefore, that the Freudian interpretation of the totem as the first beginnings of a religious concept is valid, but not as the *ideational* cause of religion. Rather, we think it mirrors primeval catastrophic economic and social events, which, in view of man's urge to explain natural processes, gave rise to religious concepts. If man in the patriarchal age created god in the image of the father, he must have formed him, earlier, on the model of his hunting animal, which naturally occupied most of his thoughts, or on the model of the primeval mother. If one reads Malinowski attentively, one finds that totemism is not nearly as important as other institutions, sexual and economic. And, after all, the degree of *importance* attached to an institution cannot be neglected if one is to fit it into a comprehensive picture of primeval organization. A thorough study of totemism must be undertaken, from the standpoint of the theory of mother-right. That can probably not be done without taking into account the unconscious meanings of religious concepts and customs, as they have so far been determined. Our criticism is directed against the method of psychoanalytical religious research hitherto practised, of drawing immediate conclusions about the origin of a religious phenomenon from its latent meaning – *of equating meaning with genesis*. To understand the origin of the present-day irrational meaning of a hysterical symptom, we must be able to fit it into the historical development of the symptom at a point where what is now irrational was entirely rational. Similarly, we must fit the latent meaning of a mythological or religious concept into the historical context of the social process: *we must understand the meaning of the religious idea from its socio-economic genesis and function*. A particular totem may well represent the father, whereas in its *origin* it was a hunting animal that only secondarily became the symbolical father- or mother-substitute.

The validity of this statement is clearly borne out by the historical development of the function of the chief. In studying primeval history, Freud, like most ethnologists, saw only that all organizations, even the most primitive, have a chief and live in families. This fact is at first confusing to the supporters of the theory of matriarchy. For this reason the other fact was overlooked – that the chief is neither sovereign nor patriarch, in our sense of those words, except where pronounced patriarchy already exists; and that the family at the beginning of history is not incompatible with the organization of self-contained clans. The family organization *within* the clan obscured the latter to the eyes of most investigators, who could not rid themselves of the theory of the *primary* nature of our present-day family and therefore thought along unhistorical lines. Just as the 'chief' fits in well with matriliny, but later comes into opposition to it because he becomes a patriarch, so the gradually evolved monogamous family organization is compatible with clan organization, but eventually, with the transformation of the chief's function, comes into opposition to it and destroys it. The refusal today to recognize the Morgan–Engels theory, which in essentials is so splendidly confirmed by Malinowski, has a sociological significance: if one clings to the primary nature of patriarchy and its form of the family, one sees compulsory morality as always having been a characteristic of man.

Morgan's discoveries, however, show that everything is constantly developing and changing. Thus, suppressive sexual morality intruded into primeval society at some point and will at some future time disappear from human society. But what takes its place?

PART TWO

THE PROBLEM OF SOCIAL
SEX-ECONOMY

SOCIAL development from primeval clan society to the present-day national state shows two interrelated processes. On the one hand, there is the development from primeval economic work-democracy to the capitalist state – i.e. the development of the means of production, the spread of and increase in production, and with it the growth of human needs and eventually the concentration of the ownership of the means of production in the hands of an upper social stratum, private capitalists or state capitalism. On the other hand, there is the development from natural, sex-economic freedom[31] and the clan consanguine family to the ideology of extramarital asceticism and lifelong compulsory monogamous marriage; and consequently, increasing restriction, repression, and distortion of genital sexuality. But if one starts from present-day economic and sexual organization and follows it backwards, one eventually gets to a point where the economic and the sexual organizations flow into each other. There we find the origin of private property and social stratification in the sexual organization of clan society, which in the course of time made possible an accumulation of possessions, produced in a primeval work-democratic way, in the chief's family. We have seen that at that time, at the very beginning of the present-day economy of goods of exchange, when the first claims of avarice and ownership interest stirred, first conflicts within human society also arose. Engels correctly writes about them:

The first class-conflict that appears in history coincides with the development of the antagonism between man and woman in monogamous marriage and the first class-suppression with that of the female sex by the male sex [Now we can say: of the woman's clan

31. This is the exact opposite of sexual libertinism due to orgastic impotence.

by the man's clan. Reich]. Monogamous marriage was a great historical progress, but at the same time it initiated, apart from slavery and private property, that epoch which has lasted to this day in which every progress is at the same time a relative regression, for the welfare and the development of the one is achieved through the misery and suppression of the other. It is the embryonic form of civilized society in which we can study the nature of the conflicts which are fully developed in the latter.

Thus in the individual family, in the cases which in keeping with their historical origin clearly show the conflict between man and woman brought about by the exclusive rule of the man, we have a miniature picture of the same conflicts and contradictions in which society, split into classes since the beginnings of civilization, has been moving, unable to solve or overcome them. (*The Origin of the Family*)

Thus, parallel with the progress in the production of goods there was a decline of sex-economic morals and culture. The natural morality of the primitive matriarchal peoples, living in sexual freedom based on gratification, was infinitely superior to the morality of our age. This is particularly apparent in the absence of antisocial sexual behaviour (rape, sexual murders, etc.). All discussions of cultural and moral progress are empty talk so long as this contrast in social development is not recognized, so long as the 'savage' is looked upon as the prototype of the 'cultureless', therefore not acceptable, sexual being. His sexual culture is judged from the point of view of a morality that identifies 'cultural' with 'pure' (= 'asexual') (cf. the fascist racial theory). Has monogamy meant progress or regression? That is an unhistorical question containing an *abstract* evaluation.

Compulsory monogamy arose out of the concentration of wealth in the hands of one person, out of the desire, as Engels writes, 'to leave this wealth to this man's children and nobody else's.' This was the reason for the demand that the woman must be monogamous. But when the development of human society is traced further back, beyond the point of common origin of wealth concentrated in the hands of one person and of compulsory monogamy, one finds social organizations that are characterized and dominated by genital love life, while production is still almost entirely undeveloped and is based on communal economy, on primitive work-democracy.[32] This type of organization is disturbed by a process consisting of the *growing restriction and suppression of genital freedom*. Its first appearance is the prohibition of the sexual embrace within one's own clan, i.e. with all maternal kin. *This process of sexual suppression is older than the 'class conflict' between man and woman* and is the *cause* of this antagonism. Traces of primeval history found in mythology point to elemental catastrophes that threatened the economic existence of primeval man and caused migrations, from which the first impulse to sexual restriction, in the form of the incest taboo, derived. The constantly increasing sexual taboos and restrictions of genitality went hand in hand with the widening of the economic interests of certain groups in primeval society. Conditions among the Trobrianders show that these are the interests of the chief's family as opposed to those of the clan. In primeval times, in essentially the same way as today, conditions of social existence gave rise to certain legal and moral institutions, such as the incest taboo within the clan, the marriage order, etc., which perpetuated themselves by ideologically pervading every individual of this society.

In accordance with Morgan's arrangement of the development of human society from savagery to barbarism to civilization, we see that the decisive turning point from primitive work-democracy to the emergence of interest in the private accumulation of goods occurred in the transition from savagery to barbarism. Its chief characteristic is the decline of matriarchal society and the evolution of patriarchal authority. Human history *before* this point is many times as long as the subsequent period of development of private economy. If, since then, the economic interests of the owners of the means of production and the opposite interests of the suppressed

32. Engels, *The Origin of the Family*. 'The less work is developed, the more restricted the number of its products, consequently also the wealth of society, the more strongly the social order appears to be predominated by sexual ties.'

have filled social life, previously it was sexual interests; if afterwards private economy determined social structure, previously kinship community did so.[33] This does not, of course, affect the fundamental fact that previously the *primitive* conditions of production were the *basis* on which a society could be built whose main interest was genitality. Apart from the fact that the individual's interests were mainly genital and were *satisfied*, the material needs were slight. Interest in property and avarice increased in proportion to the extent to which genital interests had to be suppressed. During one phase of human history, living conditions (first the union of primeval hordes, later the excessive pressure of the marriage gift) gave rise to sexual restriction and sexual repression. This freed psychic interests for a specific type of economic evolution i.e. *private economy*. These interests were avarice and the desire to accumulate, and they sprang up at the expense of the genital interests.[34]

We are confronted with the question – decisive in the history of sex-economy – whether sexual suppression is an integral part of the development of human society or belongs only to a certain economic and social stage of this development. The former is assumed by Freud and most of his disciples, and also by many Marxists (Salkind, for example). On the basis of this investigation we repudiate the idea that sexual suppression is a *necessary* component of the development of human society, because we recognize in it a mechan-

33. 'It will soon be perceived that in the initial stages of savagery, community of husbands and wives, within prescribed limits, was the central principle of the social system. The marital rights and privileges, established in the group, grew into a stupendous scheme, which became the organic principle on which society was constituted' (Morgan, *Ancient Society*).

34. Psychoanalytic ethnologists are, therefore, incorrect when they trace the culture of primitive races back to their instinctual constellation and speak, for instance, of anal-sadistic culture. In reality, the changed instinctual structures were created by the social process, first by restricting genitality and, second, by conditioning an intensification of the nongenital partial drives. The desire to accumulate has primarily a social origin but, in becoming anchored in the psychic structure, it makes use of anality that has been produced by sexual restriction.

istic view which can be refuted factually on the basis of present-day events, and historically as well. Also, the study of the relationship of the social order and the sexual order has led us to think otherwise.

Psychoanalytic research maintains that the cultural process is based on instinctual conflicts rather than on social factors. Thus it has obscured a problem in its own sphere of discipline of such importance that it cannot be overestimated. If we derive the instinctual conflict from the clash of primitive needs (hunger, genital needs) and the conditions of existence (economy, influences of nature, technique), we not only do justice to the prevailing influence of social existence but we grasp the interrelation of socioeconomic living conditions and the formation of human character structure. Also, we find an avenue of approach to both the conservative and the progressive role of the characterological processes of a society. The last section of this book is devoted to a discussion of the fundamental aspects of this problem.

But first we must give some attention to an examination of the role of character structure in the history of instinctual gratification.

INSTINCTUAL GRATIFICATION AND SOCIAL REALITY

Quite early, Engels had an inkling of the part played by sexuality in the structure and development of human society. If his views about this could not properly assert themselves, it was because his concept of sexuality only considered the function of procreation, leaving untouched the function of genital gratification. Also, at that time the process of sexual *repression*, with its social background, was unknown. Engels, who wanted to fit sexuality into his materialistic concept of history as a factor in shaping history, writes in the preface to *The Origin of the Family:*

According to the materialistic concept the ultimately decisive impetus in history is: the production and reproduction of life.

This process has a double nature. On the one hand, man produce food and provides himself with clothing, a dwelling place an necessary tools; on the other hand, he produces human being themselves, i.e. he propagates the species. The social institution under which man of a certain historical epoch and of a certai country lives are conditioned by both kinds of production: on th one hand by the development of work, on the other hand of th family.

This view can now be corrected. Man stands in a relation ship of mutuality to his fellow creatures for the purpose o gratifying two basic physiological needs: *the need for food* an the *sexual need*. The way in which society effects the grati fication of these vital needs has been dealt with exhaustively in economic writings of many different schools. Since th need for food cannot be transformed, as the sexual needs can but only gratified more or less, it does not play such an im portant part in the detailed formation of the character struc ture as do the sexual needs.

In *Capital*, in the discussion on the needs which pro duction serves to satisfy, Marx distinguishes between those that spring from the 'stomach' and those that spring from 'imagination'. Now, the needs of 'imagination', as they were called by Marx, have been shown by psychoanalytic research to be the transformations and developmental derivatives of the variable sexual impulses. They appear as '*subjective* factors'[35] in the history of mankind and society – not as the urge to propagate but as the urge to remove sexual tensions con ditioned by inner secretion[36] and outer stimuli, i.e. the *desire for sexual gratification*. The generation of offspring, which in *The Origin of the Family* Engels sets side by side with the production of food, takes place objectively, not subjectively like the production of food (for the purpose of gratifying the need for food). It is, therefore, not parallel to the production of food. As we know, it appears as a function only very late,

35. [1934] By 'subjective factor', present-day political psychology means chiefly the average psychic structure of man in a particular society. This structure itself is determined by the libidinous forces, which condition it.
36. [1952] Orgonotic, bioenergetic energy functions.

fter sexual maturity, whereas the actual parallel to the grati-
cation of the need for food, sexual gratification, appears
multaneously with it immediately after birth. Only in this
ubjective sense, as the urge to release a tension that is ex-
erienced as sexual gratification, with its sublimated trans-
ormations (inventive spirit, technical interest, scientific
esearch), may we introduce sexuality into history as a motive
ower analogous to hunger.

Just as the food instinct appears subjectively as hunger and
bjectively as a 'tendency' towards the preservation of the
ndividual, the sexual instinct appears subjectively as an urge
or sexual gratification and objectively as a 'tendency' to-
vards the preservation of the species. These 'objective ten-
encies' are not concrete facts, however, but assumptions. In
eality there is no tendency towards the preservation of the
pecies, as there is none towards the preservation of the in-
ividual. Both kinds of preservation are functions for whose
xplanation 'objective tendencies' are introduced, whereas
ctually they are secured by specific mechanisms of the
hysiological[37] apparatus. The tension in the stomach which
nanifests itself psychically as hunger produces an urge to
at, thus preserving the individual. The tension in the
rganism, especially in the genital organs, which manifests
self psychically as desire for the genital embrace (desire for
ratification, desire for pleasure), impels one to sexual ac-
vity in the genital act, thus preserving the species. The
ssumption of an 'objective tendency', then, becomes sense-
ess. Neither in the case of hunger nor in the case of genital
ratification does the individual think of self-preservation or
f the preservation of the species. We must therefore ask:

1. What are the natural processes in the gratification of
unger and sexuality? (Physiology of nutrition, sexual
hysiology, and sexual psychology.)

2. What is the structure of society? Does it safeguard the
ratification of these basic needs; does it encourage or hinder
heir gratification? (Sociological treatment of needs.)

3. If society hinders the gratification of these needs instead

37. [1952] Bioenergetic.

of encouraging it, it does so for what reason? What class or stratum is interested in so hindering gratification? (Political economy and sociology.)

Just as we should speak of the manner in which society provides for the gratification of the need for food of all its members as 'food economy', we should call *the way in which society regulates, promotes, or hinders gratification of the sexual needs* 'sex economy'. There is a regulated and an un regulated assimilation of food in the same way that there is a *regulated or unregulated sexual economy of the individual*. It depends on the attitude society with its institutions takes towards this gratification.

We must distinguish the sex-economy of the individual from the sex-economy established by society. The former, apart from the constitutional differences of individuals, depends chiefly on the sex-economy of society. Clinically, we judge whether sex-economy is regulated or unregulated by the extent to which discharge equals tension in the psychic apparatus of the average individual. Moreover, we judge it by the efforts this apparatus expends to bring about an equalization of tension and discharge. Elsewhere, I have tried to indicate these characteristics:[38] genital gratification – i.e. orgastic potency – and free-flowing work capacity (sublimation) characterize the ordered sexual household; sexual substitute gratifications, neurotic symptoms, and spasmodic work capacity (capacity depending on the process of reaction-formation) characterize the unregulated one.

The organization of social life determines the quantity and quality of the equalization of tension and discharge in the psychic apparatus. If there is a lack of social possibilities for genital gratification and sublimation, if the psychic apparatus has been distorted by educational influences to such an extent that it cannot make use of existing possibilities, if the measure of unpleasurable stimuli is too great owing to distress and want, the psychic apparatus works with substitute mechanisms

38. 'Der genitale und der neurotische Charakter', *Intern. Zeitschrift für Psychoanalyse*, 1929. See also *The Function of the Orgasm*, 2nd ed., 1948; and *Character Analysis*, 3rd ed., 1949.

that seek to bring about some discharge at any cost. The results are neuroses, perversions, pathological changes of character, antisocial manifestations of genital life, and, not least, work disturbances.

Contrary to the many economistic concepts of the social process which identify 'social basis' with technique and nature – consequently, with material living conditions alone – and relegate needs to the 'superstructure of society', it must be strongly emphasized that such a concept, being sheer economism, has nothing to do with Marxism. As in my book on the ideology of fascism, I must here remind the reader that Marx refers the fundamental needs to the 'basis'. Needs are constantly changing, it is true, as a result of progress in production, and new ones are continuously being created; but that does not alter the cardinal fact that both the fundamental needs that existed from the beginning and the needs created secondarily are 'basis' elements, 'subjective factors in history'. Marx writes in *German Ideology*, Part I: 'The presuppositions with which we begin are no arbitrary ones, no dogmas; they are real presuppositions from which we can abstract only in imagination. They are the *real individuals, their actions and their material living conditions, both the already existing ones and the ones produced by their actions.*' The sexual needs, although subject to change through the social process, are therefore elements of the 'basis', for they constitute a very essential part of the 'real individual' and decisively determine his 'actions'. The psychology and physiology of instincts consequently study these basis elements in their interrelation with other basis elements and social ideology in *the socialized individual*. Eliminating the sexual needs (as the subject and the object of history) from sociology is equivalent to eliminating the need for food, clothing, and shelter. If one adds that, essentially, the productive power – 'working power' – is transformed sexual energy, no extensive exposition is required to establish the urgency of sex-economy.

We are left with the task of arriving at a characterology and theory of work-economy on the basis of sex-economy, and of clarifying goals for pedagogy. This task can be carried out only by a society that has put into practice an economy regulating the gratification of the needs of all its members.

As sexual misery is a result of the compulsive regulation of genital life, we always come across it where considerations of compulsory monogamous marriage determine genital life. The relation of the sexual suppression of the population to the constraints in its social existence (food, habitation, cultural needs) is determined as follows. Whereas economic misery affects only a small segment of society, sexual misery encompasses all social strata. Sexual misery in the class that is economically prostrate takes a different form from that in the propertied classes, however. The misery of hunger and of bad housing conditions does not merely aggravate the sexual misery of the poor; in conjunction with severe sexual laws, it deprives them of the possibility of easing their burden, a possibility that is open and unrestricted for the propertied. If now, in analogy to the question of the gratification of hunger, we ask why authoritarian society regulates the gratification of sexual needs in this way and not in some other, denying it as it does, pressing it into such frames as compulsory marriage, even completely suppressing it until a given age as in childhood and adolescence, we find the answer in certain specific economic interests of this society. We then see that it is society based on government by armoured man that is interested in sexual suppression, because it needs it for the maintenance of two of its most essential institutions, compulsory monogamous marriage and the patriarchal family. The severe sexual misery, neuroses, perversions, sexual murders, etc., that result – along with the considerable restriction of the individual's working capacity – are a by-product, not intentionally sought by the authoritarian order, but inseparable from it. *The psychic disturbances produced in this way are the expression of a disturbed sexual economy.*[39] As long as the dynamics of psychic illnesses and neurotic character formation and their connection with sexuality were unknown, however, the history of sex-economy could not be elaborated. First, clinical discoveries in the realm of sex-economy had to be

39. See *The Function of the Orgasm*; also *Character Analysis*.

made, and indeed they sprang from the very soil of the patriarchal authoritarian sexual order, which produced neuroses and with them the means of studying and treating them.

This sexual order, however, has not always been in existence. It has evolved from other forms dating back to earlier stages of social development. Although the respective sexual economy had a considerable influence on the development of society and especially on its intellectual output, it is itself the result of a specific social regulation of the production and distribution of food.

In the history of mankind, in a way directly related to the economic interests of society, the sexual order changed from an essentially *affirmative* one that promoted human sex-economy into a *sex-negating*, suppressive one that conditions man's sexually *uneconomic* way of life. This historical event was brought about by the transformation of matriarchal into patriarchal society, of primeval work-democratic society into a society based on work as a commodity. Natural society did not know sexual suppression, any more than any other natural organization of living beings does. Not until patriarchy and the armouring of children came into being were all the economic interests created which have since provided the social basis for sex-negating morality and the consequent disturbed sex-economy. From the progressively developing phases of the dependence of man, negative sexual morality draws its right to exist and also its contradictions. It finally establishes itself in authoritarian society as a pronounced reactionary factor, becomes one of the mainstays of the church, and puts the socially suppressed into a relation of dependence to the state, also with regard to sexuality. Further, through its influence on all education in and outside the family and all sex research, it creates, from childhood, psychic structures in the mass individuals that are altogether in harmony with the interests of the ruling classes. Negative sexual morality interests us, therefore, not just in an academic-theoretical way but from a practical point of view, as it hinders the restructuring of the masses. For, through its suppression of sexuality, the patriarchal family, in addition to reproducing itself ideologically, becomes the most important ideological producer of the pillars of reactionary society, viz. hierarchy in state, church, and business. It is therefore defended in every way possible by every reactionary social philosopher and sex and culture researcher as *the* foundation of the state, making recognition of its reactionary nature difficult.

The disintegration of the compulsory family is taking place largely without conscious awareness, as one of the symptoms of the transformation of our social organization. The conscious and active guidance and promotion of this objective process of disintegration will be possible only when the sociological role of sexual suppression and repression affecting every individual has been fully recognized and the knowledge thus gained has been turned to practical preventive and educational measures.[40]

When the compulsive regulation of sex life disappears, catch phrases such as 'sexual freedom', 'sexuality is a private affair', etc. are not sufficient to enable us to understand and consciously guide the new, self-regulated sex life which then comes into existence, whether we want it or not. Chaos ensues when a society does not understand the process it is subject to at the moment, which therefore it is incapable of guiding.

What follows when the compulsive regulation of sex life disappears? Sexual chaos, says the horrified citizen admonishingly. The history of sex-economy, however, tells us that hitherto existing compulsory regulations, which failed utterly everywhere and which led to sexual chaos, give way to regulation that is not moralistic and negative but *sex-economic* and *life positive*, thus attaining real self-regulation of sex life.

Let us summarize what we have learned so far about the laws of sexual economy from our clinical and sociological study of the clash of instinctual need and social process:

1. The compulsory regulation of sex life works by means of sexual inhibitions which it anchors in the individual in

40. The goal is prevention of armouring in man from birth onwards.

childhood. These inhibitions produce an insoluble conflict. On the one hand, through sexual repression, they cause sexual stasis and thus intensify sexual needs and turn them into secondary', cruel, perverted drives which *must* be curbed. On the other hand, they transform the structure of the person, diminishing or completely impairing his capacity for gratification. As a result of this conflict, the capacity for gratification does not and cannot equal the instinctual tension, and sexual illnesses, neuroses, perversions, and antisocial modes of sexual behaviour appear as compensatory reactions.

2. In every individual the removal of these conflicts presupposes the removal of the compulsory sexual inhibition. It is replaced by *sex-economic self-regulation of sex life through sexual gratification,* which renders compulsory regulation superfluous. That is attained in the individual by the elimination of armouring and the establishment of *orgastic potency.* The sex-economic, genital sex life deprives the antisocial and morbid secondary drives of their energy through gratification of the primary needs.

3. Sexual gratification is not in opposition to the sublimation of sexual drives in work; the latter, on the contrary, presupposes the former. The relation between sexual gratification and sublimation is not a mechanical one ('the more sexual suppression, the more social achievement') but a functional one: to a certain degree, sexual energy can be sublimated. However, if the diversion goes too far, sublimation changes into its opposite, a disturbance of work capacity.

4. There are high cultures that have no repression of sexuality, particularly of genitality, but, on the contrary, avowed sex-affirmation and social assistance for the love life of their members. Sexual repression, accordingly, is not the prerequisite of cultural development and social order.

5. The compulsory regulation of sex life, and with it sexual repression, sets in at the beginning of social stratification. Compulsory marriage and family serve as safeguards of sex repression, and it is in connection with these institutions that the demand for premarital and extramarital chastity arises.

6. With sex-affirmative, i.e. life-positive, social organization

there are no neuroses, no perversions, no antisocial sexual behaviour, no neurotic work disturbances on a socially significant scale. (That provides the ethnological proof that neuroses are the expression of a disturbed sex-economy.)

7. Genital gratification under social protection from infancy onwards automatically regulates sexual sociality, but it presupposes the absence of negative sexual morality and the presence of sex-affirmative education since childhood.

8. Sex-negative morality deriving from the compulsory marriage and family situation achieves on a social scale the opposite of what is desired: neuroses, perversions, and anti-social behaviour.

9. Sex-affirmation and sex-economic self-regulation of sexuality characterize primeval clan society; the development of the patriarchal family introduces *compulsory sexual* regulation and with it the suppression of infantile and adolescent sexuality.

10. The present, twentieth-century development gradually does away with compulsory sexual regulation and reinstates sex-economic self-regulation and social protection of sex-life, on a higher level owing to natural science and a conscious sex-economy. That becomes the prerequisite for the elimination of psychic illnesses and antisocial behaviour; and, not of least importance, it becomes the foundation of enhanced intellectual development through liberation of life energy that was constricted in the severe processes of armouring.

PRODUCTION AND REPRODUCTION OF SEXUAL MORALITY

When we derived some basic elements of Trobriand sexual morality from interests of the chief and his family, we were able actually to see the development of sexual ideologies. We have to leave unanswered the question whether all or only some elements of sexual morality develop in this way. Now, let us sum up what we know about the process through which sexual ideologies come into being.

Until there is interference from economic interests, sex life governed by the laws of natural self-regulation of the pleasure-unpleasure principle. They develop into social customs, such as the *ulatile* and the *katuyausi*, which are not directed against sexual gratification but on the contrary serve to safeguard it. Sex-negating morality first appears as the demand of a group which has economic and political power, and is directed against the other members of society for the purpose of securing and increasing this power. The demand of the one who profits becomes, consequently, the morality of the one from whom the profit is derived. The *sphere of production* of morality lies in a group that has superior power.

But to maintain compulsory morality it is not enough to make a demand or a law just once. For the continued restriction of the gratification of needs by external compulsion, the new morality would have to impose and assert itself over and over again; it would continuously have to overcome resistance in every new adult member of society and thus would scarcely be able to hold its own. It has to be rooted more deeply to fulfil its social purpose completely; it must start operating in early childhood when the resistances of the ego are still easily overcome; and from an external demand of a group in society, it must become the inner morality of all members of society. How does that happen? Through the transformation of the character structure of the mass individual. This transformation takes place in the sexual sphere through fear of punishment. Fear of punishment for sexual crimes can, in the long run, suppress the sexual drive only if it removes it from consciousness; that is, if it represses it and mobilizes counterforces against it and firmly fuses them into the personality. The conflict that originally took place between a sexual ego and a sex-negating external world thus becomes, first, a conflict between an ego that is afraid of punishment and an ego that consciously demands sexual gratification, and then passes into a (temporarily) stable state in which a moral ego permanently keeps down a repressed sexual drive. The ego that was formerly pleasure-affirming has itself become sex-negating, moralistic. *Social morality has reproduced itself in the individual*. Henceforth, all individuals are

armoured; i.e. bioenergetically rigid and subject to pleasure
anxiety, which in turn makes them orgastically impotent. This
applies to all who are subject to the same sex-negating social
situation. The individuals thus transformed will consciously
influence their offspring in the direction not of their repressed
attitudes but of their moral ones. Moreover, the specific social
situation endures, incessantly reproducing the moral demands
of the ruling social strata, so that the external social pressure
continues too. Thus, sex-negation, sex-repression, and
character armouring are secured and with them the interests
of social suppression of life.

Production and *reproduction* of compulsory morality must,
then, be distinguished from each other. The former presents
itself as a 'cultural demand'; the latter, in all members of
society, as morality, i.e. as armouring. The relation of the
social basis to the ideological superstructure is, therefore, not
an immediate one. Ideologies evolve through many inter-
mediate stages, which can be outlined as follows:

1. Development of society in the direction of suppression
of biological needs and corresponding social interrelations.

2. Certain specific economic interests of a social group or
class.

3. Corresponding moral demands on the members of
society.

4. Influence of these demands on the needs of the mass
individual; restriction of instinctual gratification; generation of social fear, etc.

5. Anchoring of the moral group demands in the mass
individual through transformation of his variable needs,
through alteration of his character structure in the direction of
the new morality: constant reproduction through internaliza-
tion of the demands, making them inherent.

6. Inner acceptance of this compulsory morality by the mass
individual; character armour; individual formation of ideologies that in all mass individuals in turn become (reproduced)
compulsive social morality.

This social morality, which is rooted in all individuals and
which continually reproduces itself, exerts a conservative

nfluence on the socioeconomic basis: the exploited himself affirms the economic order which guarantees his exploitation; the sexually suppressed himself affirms or helplessly tolerates the sexual order which restricts his bioenergetic gratification and makes him sick, and he himself instinctively wards off any development which would answer his needs. Thus, compulsory morality, through the process of armouring, fulfils its socioeconomic purpose.

The manner in which reactionary society maintains sexual repression by every means at its disposal affords a good example. In order to suppress life, it refuses to abolish the abortion law, though this law no longer achieves its original purpose of producing industrial reserve armies. It opposes the dissemination of contraceptives and limits the function of sexuality to propagation; and it resists marriage reform with all its might. Now, as ever, it suppresses adolescent sexuality. It is not prepared to cope with prostitution and venereal disease because for it the 'morality' of women and girls is more important. Social sex repression and character armouring are reactionary factors of great importance, and authoritarian society cannot do without their retarding effects on the social process.

1. It powerfully backs every reactionary institution which by means of sexual fear and sexual guilt feelings deeply roots itself in the exploited masses.

2. It backs the compulsory family and marriage, which require the atrophy of sexuality for their existence.

3. It makes children subservient to their parents, and thus, as adults, subservient to the state, by creating fear of authority in the mass individual.

4. It paralyses the intellectual critical powers and the initiative of the mass individual, for sexual repression uses up much bioenergy which otherwise would manifest itself intellectually and emotionally in a rational manner.

5. It impairs bioenergetic agility in many people, makes them inhibited, and paralyses their power to rebel against social evil.

All this, taken together, means the *ideological anchoring of the existing authoritarian system in the character structure of the mass individual*, thus serving the suppression of life. This is the sociological meaning of sexual suppression in society governed by powerful political cliques. Not much education is required – only a little intellectual courage – to recognize that the powers seeking to dominate do not bring colonial peoples Christianity, clothing, and 'morality' out of cultural considerations but because they want to anchor the spirit of the coolie in the individual. Moreover, they seek to weaken people with alcohol and thus make them subservient. And this anchoring of serfdom in the character structures of primitive peoples, intended to make inspectors and police cudgels superfluous, can most successfully be implemented through the subjugation of the power springing from gratified genitality.

Since it was possible to find the sociological meaning of sexual repression, we should also be able to see the contradictions it creates, which destroy it. For, although sex repression strengthens every kind of authoritarian rule, it simultaneously undermines it through the sexual misery it produces. On the one hand, it instils in youth a characterological subservience to the adults; on the other hand, it generates the sexual rebellion of youth. The sexual crisis which has increasingly afflicted authoritarian society since the turn of the century is motivated by a need to resolve the contradictions of sexual suppression. It varies in intensity with the economic crises on which it depends. The deterioration of the masses' material position not only loosens the familial and marital fetters of sexuality but forces out the sexual needs along with the rebellion against hunger. That is the simple explanation of the 'decline of morality' in times of crisis. It is significant that during economic crises the forces of reaction intensify sex-reactionary pressure on the masses, even going as far as bloody terrorism. The Pope's message on Christian marriage promulgated at the end of 1930 bears out this link between material and sexual rebellion.[41] Another instance is the violent clash, in

41. In his Encyclical, *Casti Connubii* (Christian Marriage), Pope Pius XI made a strong restatement of the Church's traditional strictures against abortion and birth control. [*Editor*]

May 1931, of Czech state authorities and the members of hiking clubs who had been forbidden by the public prosecutor to spend the night in tents unless they had marriage certificates. Many were wounded in the clash. Here sexual reaction was manifested blatantly and for the first time in this form.

Social sexual suppression thus undermines itself by generating a steadily growing divergence between the tension of sexual needs and the external possibility of and internal capacity for gratification. Such social phenomena as so-called 'juvenile delinquency' are direct expressions of the sexual crisis. In many cases 'juvenile delinquency' involves nothing more than the genital embrace before it is legally sanctioned.

There can be little doubt that, since the beginning of the twentieth century, human society everywhere began to enter an entirely new phase of social upheaval. Life started to rebel against every kind of suppression. Unconscious of their nature and of their true goals, misled by the stupidities of an ignorant politiciandom, without leadership and therefore chaotic, the multitudes have appeared on the social scene, claiming their right *to live in happiness*. Outworn political systems may still, for a while, abuse and mislead this genuine striving of the people, but there can be no doubt whatsoever: *the sexual revolution is in progress,* and no power on earth will stop it. What it needs is rational direction towards its goals.

APPENDIX

Roheim's 'Psychoanalysis of Primitive Cultures'

ROHEIM'S METHOD OF ETHNOLOGICAL RESEARCH

In the spring of 1929 the Hungarian ethnologist and psychoanalyst Géza Roheim made an expedition to Australia and New Guinea, underwritten by Princess Mary Bonaparte. The result of this expedition, which lasted several years, is now available in a preliminary report consisting of some hundred pages.[42] The conclusions of these investigations, in so far as they do not simply render observations but go on to theory formulation, can be understood only if one grasps the fundamentals of the method Roheim applied to effect his aim of providing psychoanalytic ethnology with a 'solid base'.

Roheim undertook the expedition, as he writes, in order to invalidate those theories which, by referring to matriarchal organizations, deny the universal existence of the Oedipus complex. He seeks to establish the universal validity of this complex – that is, its *biological* character. And herein lies the root of his mistakes. He turns against Malinowski, who, on the basis of his study of a matriarchal society, maintained that the child–parent conflict that Freud investigated in *patriarchal* society shows an entirely different structure in a *matriarchal* society. I, too, on the basis of Malinowski's research, had *refuted* the biological nature of the well-known typical child–parent conflict.

Whether one applies the term 'Oedipus complex' to conflicts in which the 'educator' is not the father but the mother's brother and in which other circumstances, too, are different, or whether one then refers to an 'Oedipus complex of a different type' is of secondary importance. Roheim had started out on his journey with the intention of demonstrating

42. Roheim, *Die Psychoanalyse primitiver Kulturen.*

that the Oedipus complex in the form in which Freud found it in Europe was a universal biological fact.

Roheim now seeks to study the culture of primitive peoples by means of psychoanalytic *interpretation*, and he believes he can do this by identifying society, its culture and civilization, with an individual. To this, one must say: a social organization cannot be studied by psychoanalytic *interpretation*, for *society has no drives, no unconscious, no super-ego, no inner life*. It consists of social *interrelations between men* possessing a psychic apparatus of a certain structure. Only man's character structure can be investigated psychoanalytically, and in so far as the results of this investigation establish typical – therefore, mass-psychological – facts, they also explain the structure of the respective social ideology.

Man, it is true, shapes society and creates the social content of life, but he does so only under certain external conditions (economic, climatic, geographic, etc.). Thus, he is restricted in the expression of his will. In addition, the social interrelationships created by him become independent, with their own inherent *sociological* laws, to which man then is subject. Sociology is essentially the science of the laws of social interrelations which dominate man yet are independent of him. These laws are *external* to the psyche; they are biosocial. Those who disregard them in favour of psychic forces represent psychologism; those who rule out the psychic structure of man, as for example the Russian dictators, must be representative of economism and fall prey to a mystical sociologism.

Roheim not only denies the fundamental function of the biosocial laws; his interpretative technique is so primitive, it so strongly resembles the 'art' of the wildest analysts, that he cannot be accepted even as a psychoanalyst.

We read, in his report, that 'Just as in therapeutic analysis through the interpretation of the transference the analyst is able to reconstruct the original infantile libido organization, the ethnologically investigating analyst can see from the transference dreams (of primitive people) what is the nature of the libido-organization and of the character of a people.' First we must make a correction: we do not reconstruct the

nfantile libido-organization of our patients through interpretation, as Roheim does; our interpretation puts together
unconscious material offered by the patient and gives it the
anguage of consciousness. Without unconscious material,
here is no interpretation. Anything else is wild analysis. To
reconstruct an individual's infantile history, an actual re-
enactment of childhood in recollection and action is needed.
Roheim analyses the dreams of 'native X, but at the same time
a human society, to wit that to which X belongs.' Let us
assume for a moment that it is permissible to draw conclusions
concerning the structure of society from the structure of
dreams, instead of conversely the structure of dreams from
the structure of the society that determines the instinctual
structure of the individual. Then, free association would be
the first requisite. But the primitive, from whose dreams
Roheim – in contrast to sociologists – believes it is possible
to 'find a formula for the unconscious desire by which every
structure of society is determined, in the same way as a system
of such unconscious desires underlies every dream and every
neurosis', is not even capable of that. 'A primitive, however,
cannot possibly be induced to associate freely; nothing else
can be done but to wait until one day he does so spontaneously.' We can scarcely thank Roheim for the disservice
he has rendered psychoanalysis with his 'method of culture
research'. What a struggle it is to get patients to associate
freely so that we may reconstruct their childhoods – and
Roheim deduces a whole culture from *one* primitive who was
not willing to associate freely.

Let us reflect for a moment what purpose is served by
ethnological research and what it seeks to do, to understand
fully what Roheim proposed to accomplish through his
method. Man continuously struggles to establish a more
favourable way of life, to gain a greater mastery of nature, to
obtain some glimmer of light about his existence. With a
knowledge of past history, one hopes to be able more easily
to cope with the present. Everyday practical problems lead us
to undertake research in order to be better equipped to cope
with the future. We explore old forms of economy and of the

family in order to understand the social developments we are subject to, so that we can give them some direction and even try to master them. Roheim is above such things: 'In our opinion, all the publications of this school (the "functional school"), whether they concern canoes, marriage, magic or trade, come to the same conclusion in reverse order; to wit, that the phenomenon concerned is the structural element of a totality, that it fulfils a well-defined function in the social mechanism and acts and reacts on other social phenomena. We shall hardly be satisfied with wisdom of such self-evident nature.' To Roheim what matters is of course the famous subconscious cultural aspirations! The ethnological schools certainly suffer severely from serious defects in their methods of investigation. They rarely go beyond mere description; they see only economic relationships and then only from a psychological point of view. They cannot distinguish a single process governing social development. Also, they approach nowhere near the sex-economic question of how and through what means biosocial existence is transformed into character structure and what effects the human psychic structure that emerges has on the social relationships out of which it comes. That is a functional bioenergetic question foreign to their manner of thinking and likely to make ethnologists uncomfortable. Roheim regresses even further beyond the achievements of his colleagues: he confuses the phenomena, mystifies them, fails to notice the most obvious things, such as the biosocial function of the Mwadare as a primitive exchange of goods availing itself of the marriage relationship. He sees nothing but symbols, and thus, like all wild interpreters of symbols, betrays his deep doubt of the realities of the *psychic* processes themselves.

It will be said that I am exaggerating. On the contrary, I am endeavouring *not* to exaggerate, in the interest of the decisively significant role of depth-psychology in sociological research. I am eager to learn, from the mistakes of an ethnology specialist such as Roheim, what mistakes must be avoided and how important methodological accuracy is in historical biosocial research.

I am now going to present a dream of a primitive as related
nd analysed by Roheim, and I shall try to indicate what this
ream reveals if one refrains from 'interpreting transferences'
ut views the dream within its social environment.

The Christian chief of Loboda, Doketa, tells Roheim a
ream from which Roheim then deduces the cultural history
f Normanby Island.[43]

'I went fishing with Gomadobu. We caught a quadovara and
ulled it out. Near Bwaruada we went ashore and cut the fish open
nd it was being boiled as the church bells were ringing. Mr Walker
aid: "Leave your fish, it will wait for you; first go to church, then
eturn and eat." Then we came back and Gomadobu cut the fish
n pieces. I received the body and said: "Give it to our friends."
ut Gomadobu said: "The body is your share, I give it to you,
ur friends will get their shares later on."'

Roheim gives a complicated reconstruction of Doketa's
nfantile past, that he eavesdropped when his parents were
aving coitus, that he wanted to kill the father, etc., etc. There
 no way of determining whether Roheim's interpretation is
orrect; but that is not important from the point of view of
ultural, biosocial research. If one reads pages 305–8 of the
eport, one sees how unreliable these findings are even if
oheim had submitted Doketa to a proper analysis.

Let us try to understand the dream on the basis of the life
nvironment and the present-day conflicts of the dreamer.
We are more modest than Roheim, for we do not pretend to
each beyond the present-day, easily accessible social en-
ironment into the infantile individual conflicts of Doketa,
ho does not himself provide any recollections. Yet a rough
nowledge of present-day causes can lead to an under-
tanding of the *present-day* conflicts reflected in the dream. We
hall see, too, that the latent meaning of the dream provides
lements such as no European can produce.

Malinowski's investigations, on which I base the eth-
ological foundations of social sex-economy, give evidence

43. Off the eastern tip of Papua, not far from the Trobriand Islands.
Editor]

that primitives suffer from two serious, typical conflicts deriving from the beginnings of change in the social organization. They are conflicts, then, which cannot always have existed and which, with the further transformation of the social organization, will, of necessity, also change their content and form. One conflict, an economic one, is the *pressure of the marriage tribute* exercised by one clan on the other. This seemed to me a preliminary stage of the later condition of private economy of exchange of goods. Roheim gives a highly accurate description of the exchange of marriage gifts and of the accompanying emotional conflict, though he has no inkling of what he is in fact describing. The yearly marriage tributes are paid under pretence of the greatest friendship, as gifts of love, but they are accompanied by wild ritual insulting of the receiver of the gift.

In his book, *Die Psychoanalyse primitiver Kulturen*, Roheim describes the distribution rite among the Papuas in the Duau district. Not only does it tally in essence with what Malinowski described; it supplements our knowledge of the psychic conflicts accompanying the payment of the marriage tribute.

'There is no doubt,' Roheim writes, 'that the distribution of goods (food distribution) is the paramount symptom of Papuan civilization in the Duau district.' The Mwadare is a festival given either by the husband's sister in honour of his wife or by his wife in honour of his sister. It consists of a complicated ceremonial in which garden produce is handed over. The entire clan participates in the formal presentation, in the background. The Mwadare is essentially a ritual exchange of goods between two different totem groups, the husband's sister representing one clan, his wife the other. Officially, these festivals of the delivering up of goods are meant to give the two clans entering into a marriage relationship an opportunity to manifest mutual good will. The two groups outdo each other in generosity, but mutual suspicion and hatred are evident in every detail of the ceremony. Roheim's informant said: 'Mwadare Gidemusa sei ja'; that is, the Mwadare is like a war in which each fighter has his special adversary. How heavy a burden the tribute is for the clan that pays is attested by the songs that accompany the rituals. Whereas every effort is made not to seem stingy, to give an especially rich Mwadare, the songs express the exact opposite, the ardent desire that the yam hut may not be large, the yam piles smaller, etc. One song goes:

> *Boe Kotona*
> Hero the nape of his neck
> *Janoujama*
> I have pulled back
> *Janu hetu hetunani*
> I pull to make it shorter
> *Ni Ketaurina*
> This filling (with yams)
> *Tuna heta siwenaja*
> Full it overflows
> *Ija, ija, ijo, ijo.*

With this song, which openly expresses the wish that the yam house may be smaller so that it may be filled more easily, the festival is initiated. The filling of the yam house is accompanied throughout by songs reflecting anxiety and mourning, detailing catastrophes and the wish that children may not be born, etc. At the end, according to Roheim, who was an eyewitness, a great quarrel arises, all in the form of ceremonial songs, in which the two parties seemingly make serious reproaches, saying that the produce is not good and is not plentiful; counter-reproaches follow. 'Mwadare is like war.'

The second conflict, a sex-economic one, concerns the *restriction of genital freedom*. Through the development of the patriarchal family organization, and even more cruelly through the actions of the church, which consciously eradicates the high sexual culture of the primitives in order to anchor mystical faith, this restriction at some point becomes complete. The sexual conflict is clearly expressed in the dream; the economic one is only hinted at. I do not know what part fishing plays in the economy of Loboda. Maybe none. What is in any case clear is that the choice of the penis symbol (fish) is not accidental. Everywhere – in our society, too – social conditions are largely responsible for the symbol chosen. A primitive is hardly likely to use an umbrella or a dirigible as a symbol of the male organ, nor a sausage; but much more often than a Central European he will use the fish, especially if fish is his staple diet. That is decisive; for what Roheim seems unaware of is that in clinical analysis it is of no importance that a certain symbol signifies the penis. That is easy to determine. What is important is why the dreamer has chosen this symbol and no other. If Roheim had asked himself this question, he would have spared psychoanalysis the ridicule he exposes it to in his book. For example, 'The fish was being boiled as the church bells were ringing': Roheim makes no comment whatever on the 'church bells', *the foremost experiential element among a primitive people which has only recently come to feel the pressure of the church* against happiness in the genital embrace. Yet this is the most significant element of the dream for an understanding not only of the culture of the country but of the effect the coming of the church had on the character structure of the inhabitants. In *this* connection, and only in this connection, can we understand part of the dream. The meaning is this: when our penis is being 'boiled', then the church bells begin ringing – that is, when we are excited genitally and want to obtain gratification, the clergy-man calls us to church; he keeps us from having our happiness: 'Go to church first.' The boiling of the penis is a sign of sexual excitation, comprehensible and significant only in this connection. Roheim correctly discerns that he, himself, is identified with the clergyman, also that the primitive feels aggression towards him; but since he does not know the social situation, he overlooks the fact that this aggression is immensely significant, that, for the primitive, he represents the whole of white culture, which the primitive hates and at the same time fears. Roheim is only interested in the fact that the primitive 'directs his aggression against himself'. 'He tells me that he has kept some magic remedies for me.' No, the primitive consciously hates the clergyman; he *is afraid of* Roheim (hence, no associations with the dreams) and tries to *cheat* him by appeasing him, by making a confession to him.

He knows only too well that the whites are keenly interested in magic remedies, but he does not want to be robbed of them. Deep down, his behaviour must presumably be traced back to fear of punishment for sexual activity. We do not wish to make the same mistakes Roheim made, however, and so will stop here.

The first conflict, the socioeconomic one (undoubtedly bearing a relationship to castration), emerges in the part of the dream that deals with the *division of the fish*. Doketa himself – though Roheim does not notice it – touches upon the subject of the *marriage tribute*, the sociological elucidation of which Roheim so strongly resents.

Besides, everyone knows that it is high time the Sagari (festive distribution of yams) for Lobesenni (the father-in-law) was prepared. But he withholds it from him because he needs the yams of his own garden for the funeral repast of his sister ... As long as possible, he keeps the magic remedies back from me, just in the same way as he keeps back the produce of his garden from his father-in-law. In the dream this is represented by the opposite: generously he offers his friends the best part of the fish.

The reversal in the dream reflects a reversal in the life of these primitive people, and behind it a social tragedy: the first economic compulsion of mankind, the payment of marriage tribute. (I do not know, because Roheim does not mention it, whether the tribe is still matriarchally oriented or is already patriarchal. I am inclined to assume the latter; otherwise, Doketa as a husband would not have to provide his father-in-law with marriage tribute but would himself receive it from his wife's brother, as among the Trobrianders.) We therefore see that *the social structure of society is reproduced in a specific manner in the character structure of the primitive of this society*, and with it the prevailing moralistic ecclesiastical system.

Since Roheim set out on his expedition with the preconception of an unalterable, eternal child–parent conflict that takes the same form at all times and in all places, he not only did not learn anything about the specific differences between the structure of the primitive and our own, which would of course be very instructive, but he overlooked the most important elements of social organization. Doketa's individual conflicts are of little interest *ethnologically*. What would be significant for a different psychology of mass structure are the *typical* differences. If only Roheim had learned something about those, we would have reason to be indebted to him. But he remarks: 'According to my present view, it will be possible at some future time on the basis of similar investigations to draw up a psychological classification of mankind and to arrange the single peoples according to degrees of primitiveness.'

Not only will that *not* be possible with this method, but it will make psychoanalysis entirely useless as an instrument of ethnology: 'culture springs from the genitofugal libido-current.' It is interesting for the biosociologist to see how any thesis of this sort goes wrong and just hangs in mid-air. If it were not for the fact that psychoanalysis is a splendid instrument for research and that Roheim himself involuntarily touches upon an important new point without knowing it, we would not take the trouble to consider his interpretations.

In the winter of 1926 Roheim visited me and we discussed ethnological problems for a few hours. We did not understand each other in one essential point, among others. We talked of the interpretation of symbols and, in connection with that, of the analytic interpretation of the origin of tools. I maintained that an axe was originally created for rational motives – *secondarily*, it might acquire a symbolic meaning, but not *necessarily* so. A tree or a stick *might* signify a phallus in a dream, but it did *not have to*. The wrong application of symbol interpretation only helped the opponents of psychoanalysis, particularly in so far as biosocial, rational activity was concerned. Airplanes were built so that man might better contend with time and space; the fact that in dreams they become phallic symbols is important only for the psychology of an individual, not sociologically. Roheim, however, believed that an axe was a penis symbol, that it was created as such, that the rational function was secondary, that therefore the making

of tools of production was nothing but a projection of unconscious symbolisms. I owe to this discussion a fruitful
clarification of the relationship of the rational to the irrational
which I formulated some years later.[44] At the same time, I
became aware of the unbridgeable gap between metaphysical
and scientific psychoanalysis. Fundamentally, the conflict still
centres around the question whether an axe is merely a symbol
of the penis and nothing but that, or, at most, secondarily a
tool of production; or whether the motive for making an axe is
primarily a rational one – to master a part of the world. And
behind this disagreement about 'the nature of the axe' there
is the embittered conflict of two viewpoints of the world that
cannot exist side by side without friction. Only *one* of them
can be correct, that is, can comprehend the world correctly
and master it. This disagreement is at the root of a conflict,
costing millions of human victims – the conflict between a
functional, natural-scientific concept of the world and a
metaphysical, fascist, dictatorial, mystifying one.[45] It is a
question of whether or not Roheim is right in summing up
his criticism of my ethnological investigation[46] in the sentence:
'It is not as Reich thinks, that civilization (= capitalism) arises
from some economic cause or other and then produces the
neurosis, but the other way round; the collective neurosis
explains, conditions and creates social organization, religion,
economy, law and all the rest.' And where does the 'collective
neurosis' come from? Apparently from the everlasting.

Roheim maintains that culture originates from the '*genito-
uga l libido-current*'.

Where does the libido-current of culture flow?
What causes this flow?
When and how did it begin?

44. In *Dialektischer Materialismus and Psychoanalyse*, II, Auflage, 1934
(Verlag f. Sexualpol.).
45. [1951] The most efficient exponents of the latter view today are the
political prostitutes who took over the once great thoughts of Karl
Marx.
46. Roheim, in a review of *Der Einbruch der Sexualmoral* (*Intern. Zeitschrift für Psychoanalyse*, 1934).

What is the difference between this flow among the Trobrianders and in America?

If these questions remain unanswered, Roheim thereby admits that he has merely manipulated words. He must be able to offer concrete reasons for such a categorical sentence in a scientific paper claiming to put ethnology on an entirely new basis.

I tried to formulate concretely what Roheim here vaguely suspects, or *perhaps* vaguely suspects, for his book does not show any signs of it. I maintained that in the beginning, by nature, there is no restriction on sex life, because natural phenomena cannot impose it. Sexual suppression, which produces a retrogression, a tendency to withdraw from the genital, is generated by elements of biosocial development. New economic interests, gradually emerging, make the sexual suppression of children desirable to economic profiteers. Thereby, the members of the society gradually change; they acquire a different structure. *Sex-affirmation turns into sex-negation*, and a 'genitofugal direction of the libido' arises – to wit, *fear of sexuality in human beings, not in the culture*. And the same human beings who had created a culture on the basis of sexual and economic freedom now establish a new culture of sex-negation, with all its consequences, such as rejection of happiness in life in general. They create an ideology and moralistic structure in which there is no room for libido-currents of any sort, for neither society nor culture has a body and a vegetative nervous system in which such things can occur. *The biosocial process consequently has transformed man through the transformation of his sexual structure; and man, thus transformed, shapes economy and culture in a different way, maintaining class division, sexual suppression, life negation, etc.*

There is, consequently, a 'retrogression in culture', but it can only be comprehended and mastered if first its biosocial basis and then its psychic reproduction is understood. This latter appears as an inhibition of the genito-libidinous powers of man in the culture in question. It compels him either to fall back to earlier forms of culture or to develop other forms of the inhibition of cultural development, mostly mystical ones (e.g. the mysticism of national-socialist ideology in German and Russian state imperialism).

Roheim, however, is very proud of his ethnological application of psychoanalysis, though he makes mistakes even in dealing with individuals. He disputes Malinowski's right to maintain that he has applied psychoanalysis in ethnology.

Although Malinowski himself does not claim to be an analyst, all the same some of his statements regarding analysis might give rise to gross misunderstandings. Thus he mentions, for instance, that while living among the Trobrianders he received some of Freud's publications from Prof. Seligman and thereupon set about trying out the correctness of Freud's theory of dreams on the Trobrianders. A person admitting that so far he has never analyzed a dream – and that for the plausible reason that he did not know how to do so – wants to check Freud's theories!

Ignorance is here joined with a poorly justified lack of modesty. I met Malinowski personally in December 1933; till then I knew him only through his writings. If Malinowski admits that he has never analysed dreams and only read Freud's publication on the Trobriand Islands; if Roheim, on the contrary, boasts that he is *the* long-experienced psychoanalyst and that he interprets dreams brilliantly – then everything speaks for Malinowski and against Roheim. For in his research Malinowski has made splendid use of psychoanalytic knowledge, and Roheim has from the beginning made catastrophic use of it. From reading Malinowski one can learn really new facts and ideas, whereas Roheim merely gives rise to confusion. We shall see what that implies.

WILD INTERPRETATION, HENCE GROTESQUE EXAGGERATION OF THE USUAL ERRONEOUS VIEWS

The life-negative concept of sexuality, if it goes beyond mere description to the formulation of a philosophy of life, maintains that: men are the born masters of women; children should be spanked for any sexual activity; sadism is natural in man, masochism in woman; women are passive in sexual experience, men are active; jealousy, which finds expression in murder and in the tormenting and embittering of life, is a natural phenomenon characteristic even of protozoa and certainly of animals in general; sexual suppression in childhood and puberty is the most natural thing in the world, also the bio-pathies and neuroses resulting from it. Roheim not only attempts to confirm ethnologically the absolute nature of these things, he exaggerates them into the grotesque. His views are important to us because they reveal the mentality of a type of research which makes a show of being objective but in reality is corroded by the severest sexual inhibitions and reactionary tendencies. They throw into bold relief the un-scientific procedures of moralistically prejudiced researchers which otherwise are covered over and difficult to see.

Let us review some instances of this 'objective' research:

In dealing with the Pitchentaras, Roheim interprets incest-fantasies from stories, and maintains – something we can neither confirm nor refute – that 'masturbation is tied to subconscious incest-fantasies'. He goes on to say:

Considering these incestuous masturbation-phantasies, one might expect to learn something about threats of castration directed against masturbation. But that would be erroneous. Nobody objects to children masturbating and I have often seen Tankaj playing with the penis of her son Aldinga. [As our mothers are in the habit of doing, only neurotically and unconsciously. W.R.] Also my direct question as to the existence of threats of castration was answered in the negative; nevertheless, I think that this information is not correct and that my informants had repressed their recollections of threats of castration.

I have offered sociological reasons for the origin of the fear of castration that destroys our children and adolescents, body and mind – without looking for a justification in these reasons, as Roheim does.

It does not occur to Roheim that character structures can exist which do not include a fear of castration, for he regards this fear as biological.[47] And when, later, to save his position, he emphasizes that he has often heard children playfully threatening to tear out each other's penises, he merely confirms a view which I maintain clinically: that it is not *important whether an idea exists* per se, *but solely whether it is bioenergetically charged and thus becomes pathological*. That also applies to the incest fantasy; it assumes importance only when it acquires driving power owing to general sexual inhibition.

I have found that what today is merely a threat, implemented only indirectly, in more subtle forms, was once practised in a literal sense, for pubertal circumcision betrays its function as a means of preventing pubertal sexual activity. It is not universal, does not occur in matriarchal tribes, but emerges in incipient patriarchy, together with the restriction of pubertal genitality and the interest in compulsory marriage on the part of the woman's father. This is the core of the function to which all manner of religious and other implications have been ascribed. Roheim describes the infibulation of girls among the already *patriarchal* Somali; one may here read with what inexorable cruelty genital sexuality is destroyed. His informant supplies the reason for it.

If we did not have this custom we should never know whom we were getting. For the girls go about freely and do as they please. On the wedding-night the husband has to open the vagina (which was previously sewn up) ... This coitus which is terribly painful for the woman has to be enforced ... This weakness of the man (not to be capable of doing so) is looked upon as a great disgrace, as an avowal of impotence.

Sex-economy demonstrates that the patriarchal customs of the wedding night have nothing to do with natural love

47. In order to prevent any misunderstanding: Every animal is afraid of bodily harm, especially harm that would affect the pleasure-giving organs. In this sense, the fear of castration is universal. But when in psychoanalysis we speak of fear of castration we mean something different: not so much the rational fear which appears whenever the genital is really threatened, but the *neurotic fear* regarding the penis which has no present-day rational cause, but which was well justified in the past. The former will never bring about disturbances of potency, but the latter regularly does.

life, that in authoritarian patriarchy the genitality of men is considered a proof of potency, while the genitality of women is basically a disgrace. It notes that things are different among the matriarchal peoples and inquires into the causes of the change. For Roheim, the superior 'psychoanalytical' ethnologist, such questions are too 'superficial', too simple; he is concerned only with 'deep' research. Here are the results, and we quote Roheim:

We therefore see that the operation achieves a doubling of the hymen: 'Twice the woman bleeds, once when the husband cuts through the sutures with his knife, the second when he perforates the hymen with the penis.' It must therefore be assumed that the virgin as a sexual object has a specially great importance for the Somali, as he tries to preserve the woman's virginity by an operation of such a traumatic nature and with the ultimate aim of doubling the hymen.

Very true! Only, in reality, such treatment of the woman *destroys* her genitality just as thoroughly as it generates hatred for the man. Roheim continues: 'Thus the assumption seems to me to be justified that this doubly stressed virginity of the bride means a double negation of the mother, a negation of the child-bearer and the castrating queen.'

We ask ourselves how this negation of motherhood (let us not forget that Roheim, after all, is concerned with social processes) fits in with patriarchy's supreme interest in unsexual motherhood, in killing woman's genitality in order to make her especially willing to bear children. We know what part it plays in the structure of oppressive society, in its slavery and deprivation of sexual rights, to what extent the patriarchal sexual ideology of black and red fascism depends on these concepts. Roheim now tells us how he interprets this phenomenon:

When women want to inflict wounds on the vagina, they express the fact that they themselves feel the vagina is a wound in which the man's flesh putrifies. In order to do away with this fear, the vagina must disappear . . . and the woman's penis is the clitoris which as a preparation for normal sex-life is cut off.

Now we know how a woman is brought to the height of
sexual happiness: by the excision of the clitoris!

Thus for the man the infibulation actually means a complete
destruction of the sexual object: Through the suture the vagina
disappears; through the cutting off of the clitoris the woman's penis
also.

We thought Roheim had said that the man wanted to
preserve the sexual object, and here we have the exact
opposite! Perhaps Roheim believes that this is an expression of
ambivalence. He believes even more than that: *even phylogenetic and ontogenetic development requires the operation.*

Before we ask why the man needs such a destruction of the
sexual object, we must attempt to understand the operation from
the woman's point of view. It is, however, to be mentioned above
all that the operation is fundamentally a dramatically abridged
repetition of the phylogenetic and ontogenetic development. The
woman is to give up her clitoris-erogeneity and proceed to vaginal-
erogeneity.

Sic! We bow to this profound scholarship which, quite
unprejudiced, was able to plumb the deepest secrets of
phylogeny and ontogeny. Roheim also makes conclusive
statements about the sexual psychology of women: 'One
could therefore think that the operation promotes the right
attitude of women in sex-life.' (!!)

In a sense, Roheim is correct. This operation indeed promotes the 'right' attitude of women in sex life. Only two
words are missing, and those two words make all the difference: '– in patriarchy'.

Although Roheim cannot be concerned with the differences
between patriarchy and matriarchy and does not even like to
have them mentioned, the question is justified: If this operation is an expression of profound phylo- and ontogenetic
laws, why do we not find it among the Trobrianders? Or are
they phylogenically different from the Somali? This is essentially the same question I once asked Krische, who maintained that 60 per cent of all women were, *through nature's
foresight, given an insensitive vagina* so that childbearing might be

painless. The remaining 40 per cent were apparently over-looked by nature.

Such were the ideas that governed sexology at the turn of the century.

In my comparison of matriarchal and patriarchal organization and the transition of the former into the latter, I found that with the economic interests of a developing upper social stratum and the suppression of the sex life of children and adolescents, the sexual experience of the whole community changed. Sexual disturbances and neuroses appeared – sadistic attitudes in the sex life of the men and sex negation in the women – which in turn necessitate artificial measures for the re-establishment of destroyed sexuality. Thus, a clinical fact which is systematically hushed up because it upsets many concepts was ethnologically confirmed. Sadism in sex life is as prevalent as it is today only when the natural genital functions are hindered or disturbed; in other words, *inhibited genitality changes not only into anxiety but also into sadism, and perhaps this is the sole origin of sadism* – a statement which is certainly important for the prophylaxis of neuroses. But Roheim and most analysts view sadism as a natural manifestation in the area of sex, and its origin is therefore biological. As a result, not only is individual development squeezed into rigid biological formulae, which bars any possibility of prophylactic measures, but also ethnology must be brought in to help. Instead of asking why things are different among different peoples, why sexual sadism is non-existent in one place and so marked in another (as Roheim himself reports), he proclaims with scientific authority:

We know that the deepest sadistic attitude is tied up with the first appearance of the teeth and that it has as a sexual aim the eating up of the partner. Now we see with this people where the men's general attitude to women is so much influenced by sadism that for them the most important preparation for sexual intercourse is a square meal, symbolically presumably the eating up of the woman.

I am no ethnologist, it is true, nor have I been able to make an expedition, but I believe my view is correct in considering the eating rite of married couples – a rite not existing among the unmarried, at least for the Trobrianders – a symbol of the marriage and the *economic* unity of marriage. As we know, the conditions of economic production are expressed sexually to a far larger extent among primitive peoples than with us.

Also, instead of comprehending the fact that 'every husband beats his wife' as a sociological problem and discovering its origin, because the beating of the sexual partner is certainly not a universal phenomenon and does not occur everywhere, Roheim betrays his completely reactionary outlook on life in the following sentences:

> In the purely physical sense their manner of carrying out intercourse seems to be more genital than the European's. They penetrate more deeply, work with stronger physical stimuli; *with a slight exaggeration, one might even say that the woman is only satisfied if after intercourse she falls ill with an inflammation.*

With a *slight* 'exaggeration'? Has psychoanalysis been founded, the existence of the unconscious discovered, the morbid sadistic concept of coitus revealed, in order that an official representative of psychoanalysis may summon up the courage, and the narrow-mindedness, to assert such things with authority?

The supporters of 'free scientific research' will probably make neutral statements about this and say that they cannot prevent people from saying what they think. We know, however, that they are not at all tolerant towards life-affirmative researchers but, on the contrary, are highly dictatorial. Besides, so-called freedom of research must not be confused with libertinism.

ROHEIM REFUTES HIMSELF AND CONFIRMS THE INVASION OF COMPULSIVE SEXUAL MORALITY

Occasionally Roheim renders observations in a plain and undistorted manner. Where he does so, he refutes himself and confirms my concepts in social sex-economy.

Clinical insight into the effect of external suppression of infantile sex life induced me to doubt the biological nature of the so-called period of sexual latency. There are children in our cultural circles who do not show a significant reduction of sexual agility between the ages of seven and twelve. And if it is true, as is suggested by clinical investigation, that, in children who seem less sexual externally at this age, sexual dynamics subconsciously go on being operative, then Freud's assumption of a *biologically* given 'dichronous beginning of sex life' separating man from the animals must be revised. The *absence* of the latency period in many children in itself refuted the biological explanation. It is permissible then to conclude that *educational* influences are responsible for the occurrence of sexual latency. Ethnological research alone made a final judgement possible. Malinowski's investigations confirmed my view of the *social* origin of the latency period, for among Trobriand children, who – with the single exception of brother–sister incest – live without sexual restrictions, there *is no interruption or even lessening of sexual agility*. Latency, therefore, is brought about by the first great series of repressions during the first puberty – i.e. in the fourth to fifth year of age – which result from the severe genital denial of infantile self-satisfaction and infantile genital play at this age. This undermined Freud's assumption that the origin of neuroses is also conditioned biologically by the 'double beginning of sex-life'. Thus, too, the assumption of a phylogenetic readiness for sexual repression was put in doubt. This theory had never acquired any concrete substance anyway. Yet it was the germ of the concepts of the biological nature of sexual repression that took up more and more space in the work of the English psychoanalytic school and blocked any avenue of approach to the *sociology* of sexual repression. It is obvious, however, that the nature of sexual latency in our children and of sexual repression is not an academic but a practical problem in every sense of the word. If both phenomena are essentially biological, there is no basis for a prophylaxis of neuroses, and thereby the therapy of neuroses also takes on a pessimistic cast. But, if they are, in essence, socially conditioned, the problem of the prophylaxis of neuroses is closely related to social sexual economy. My investigation into the intrusion of compulsive sexual morality is essentially a theoretic elucidation and an ethnologic basis for the future prophylaxis of neuroses. As little had been heard in psychoanalysis about this as about the theory that sexual repression has a socioeconomic origin.

Now, Roheim reports plainly and straightforwardly – though he is not aware of the significance of what he says – that *the primitives of Central Australia are distinguished from us by the absence of the latency period.* I am convinced that, in spite of this, he is unshaken in his faith in the biological nature of this phenomenon, for were he to abandon that premise, he would have to change his entire basic attitude.

On the basis of clinical facts, I have begun to doubt the concept, prevalent in psychoanalytic theory today, that the instinctual structure is fixed by heredity and thus represents the constitutional basis of neuroses. According to this concept, an oral or anal sexual zone, for example, which quantitatively is particularly strongly developed constitutes the hereditary basis of a tendency to a depressive and compulsion-neurotic illness. Here, too, a clinical study of the psychic illnesses involved first gave rise to justified doubts as to whether this biological concept was entirely correct. There can be no doubt, that there are *differences in the excitability of the various erogenous zones* which are fixed by heredity. But there can be as little doubt that it is not the propensity in itself which determines whether a person will fall ill or not, but the combined effect of *tendency and experience* – and not in the sense of Freud's 'complementary series' constituted by tendency, infantile experience, and present-day experience. According to Freud, tendency and experience interact as absolute quantities complementing each other. If the neurotic instinctual tendency is strong, a slighter pathogenic experience is sufficient to produce the neurosis; if the former is weak, numerous and more intense educational influences are required. To me, the relationship seems to be one of *variable* quantities, i.e. functional. In the first place, it can be demonstrated that there are persons with a strong pregenital tendency who show no neurotic effects. Then, an observation of the change in the libidinous structure in character-analytic treatment shows the interdependence of the various erogenous sources. A tendency which manifests itself as a strong anal zone *can disappear when, after the elimination of the genital repression, the respective excitation is discharged.* The excitations consequently are in inter-communication and above all depend on the regulation of the total sexual economy. It could, furthermore, be seen that a good part of what, for instance, was ascribed to an anal tendency was the result of the anal-erotic character of the compulsive mother. If a mother insists that her child be completely clean, at whatever cost, by the age of six months, she may well be referring later to an 'anal disposition' as an explanation of why the child has fallen ill with a compulsion neurosis. It also became clear that the *intensity of the various erogenous zones is influenced socially by the nature, speed, and intensity of educational measures.* Supposing a society existed which allowed the child to suck at its mother's breast up to the development of the genital phase, then we might expect such children not to show any anal reaction-formations or any symptoms of an anal nature, simply because they would not go through an anal phase in our sense. Yet the Trobrianders are very clean. This proves that anal cleanliness is not of necessity a reactive formation, as it is with us.

As a result of these considerations, quite a few theories came into question. The most important conclusion was that an upbringing which presses all children into a fixed system of renunciation, irrespective of *instinctual intensity,* produces conditions which seem to be tendencies. *A child who, on the whole, generates less energy can more easily adapt itself to the same situation of renunciation than a child who generates more energy.* If, then, the latter becomes 'nervous', a hundred psychiatrists out of a hundred conclude that they are dealing with a 'nervous-degenerative-tendency'. *A greater production of energy in a biological system is, however, no nervous tendency.* If the psychic energy of the different individuals in the younger generation had sufficient scope to find its own level. if these young people were not subject to a uniform ideology and education, the stronger 'instinctual organization' would not appear as a 'nervous tendency'; the child who generates greater bio-energy would merely romp about more vigorously than a child with lesser energy and it would masturbate every second night instead of every fourth as a weaker one does. In a family of five children, all of whom have to be *equally* 'good', quiet, and controlled, the reaction of the different children clearly must differ. I believe this premise is sound and refutes a number of assumptions concerning heredity. Thus, *we do not deny heredity, but we assess it by the degree of energy production in the biological system.* Then one can understand that the very persons who are deemed psychopaths and morally insane by narrow-minded heredity research prove themselves, in character analysis, to be the *richest* in energy, the *most intelligent* and *agile*. But they do not fit into this life-negative society and therefore have a difficult life. When, in Hitler Germany, fifteen-year-old girls who have boyfriends are condemned to sterilization as psychopaths, we look at it from a different point of view than Roheim.[48]

I wanted to show how important such controversies are for the weal and woe of generations. It is therefore not im-material whether a prominent representative of psycho-analysis derives correct or incorrect data from his voyage of exploration. Roheim considers the instincts to be absolute and believes that their suppression has a biological origin. That supports irrevocably the laws on sterilization of psycho-paths and schizophrenics whom a rotten social order itself produces. Roheim, however, reports that anal-reactive characteristics are entirely absent in the primitive cultural circles he explored – and sadomasochistic perversions too. Roheim is undoubtedly a keen advocate of the theory of the original nature of sadistic aggression. *How does he explain its absence in entire cultures?* Since Roheim considers it superfluous to describe and discuss the economic and social structures of the organizations he studied, his positive findings are useless.

48. [1951] We also judge the red fascist elimination of co-education from this bioenergetic point of view.

Malinowski's findings, however, afford far-reaching insights, among them that the development of natural aggression into sadism presupposes the social inhibition of natural genital sex life in the masses of a society. That applies both to the sadistic alteration of the structure of the individual and to the existence of a sadistic sexual ideology. The central mechanism of this social evolution is the interest in permanent compulsory marriage which has developed from loose pairing marriage. In it one sees for the first time the sadistic behaviour of men towards women. This does not exist otherwise and is therefore not biological as Roheim believes.

IS INFANTILE ANXIETY SOCIALLY OR BIOLOGICALLY CONDITIONED?

That the anxiety which our children regularly develop is caused by unsatisfied inner bioenergetic impulses is generally known and accepted today. For the problem of the prophylaxis of neuroses it is of decisive importance to determine *what* is responsible for the failure to master *instinctual impulses*. Here opinions differ, and not in the sense of 'not only/but also' but of 'either/or'. Freud traces anxiety back to the reaction of the ego to external or internal dangers and holds that every anxiety represents a repetition of the traumatic experience of birth. The English psychoanalytic school maintains that the anxiety of the small child is fixed biologically in the weakness of the infantile ego, which is not equal to the powerful instinctual drives and has to defend itself from them by repression. We ask, however: if anxiety represented a repetition of the anxiety of birth, would it not of necessity affect all children – *those of the Trobrianders too* – as though it were an expression of the biological imperfection of the ego?[49] If this does not apply, however, it is important to know what it is that determines whether or not the child's ego will lag behind its drives, whether or not it will reproduce the birth situation. Freud abandoned his thesis that anxiety is the expression of inhibited sexual excitation. I consistently worked

49. Cf. my view on birth anxiety, in *The Function of the Orgasm.*

on this assumption, for it is the only one that makes sense, the only one that is correct. It permits the further thesis that it must be external circumstances and experiences – i.e. social factors – which condition the transformation of sexual excitation into anxiety. That means that we include social sexual economy in our theory of neuroses, whereas the theories outlined above not only rule it out but present themselves as theses advanced *ad hoc* for the purpose of avoiding the biosociological approach. In addition, my theory has the advantage that it does not depart from the central concept of the conflict between need and world, but fully fits in with it and carries it further.

When we thus confront the biological and the sociological theory, additional differences become clear. The biologic concept of anxiety does not inquire into the social origin of or the differences in infantile experience in different social organizations. For that reason, its work is easier. But it has no answer when a social organization is found in which children have *no* anxiety. Such social organizations supply us with the decisive, practical approach to the problem of the prophylaxis of neuroses, at the core of which is the problem of infantile phobia. For when we compare them with our organization, they reveal the broad outlines of the conditions under which infantile anxiety, and with it the crux of the formation of neuroses, can be avoided. And all analysts agree that anxiety, as an expression of active but blocked bioenergy, is the central problem of neuroses.

Roheim, in spite of himself, also confirms my views on anxiety. Not only does he describe the experiences of the 'fearless sons and daughters of the wilderness'; he also details quite exactly the relationship between the child's anxiety and its sex life, without suspecting the importance of what he says.

If I call these children (among the Arada, Luritjia, Pitchentara and Jumu) 'fearless', I do so quite consciously, although I know that strictly speaking they are not entirely free from experiences of anxiety.

Of course not! What living being is free from anxiety? Surely it is a question of distinguishing between *neurotic* anxiety and *rational* anxiety! If the children in certain social organizations are free from neurotic anxiety, we are then faced with the question: What factor causes children in other social organizations to become anxious and neurotic?

Roheim describes in detail a genital game that children played quite openly; essentially, it represents the genital embrace. He does not go further into the relative frankness with which the children demonstrated the genital game to him, but arbitrarily introduces into the game the Oedipus complex he has brought with him from Europe. What ensues demonstrates precisely what sex-economy has discovered: the introduction of a social restriction in the sexual life of the children, and with it a far-reaching change in their character structure.

What follows now is a compelling representation of the Oedipus complex not to be surpassed for its clearness. The little boy takes a snake and puts it at the monkey's breast. 'The snake drinks milk.' Then he squeezes the snake between the monkey's legs. 'The snake has coitus with the monkey.' An incident which took place two months later makes it perfectly clear that Depitarinja himself is the snake having intercourse with the milk-giving woman; that is, the mother.

That is of no interest whatever. That the children of the wilderness, too, desire coitus with their mothers and fathers is a matter of course; there is no doubt of it. What is of decisive importance is *whether the inhibition of this desire has a pathological effect even if children have complete freedom among themselves*. Sex-economy maintains that the *inhibition of the incest wish has no pathogenic effect if the child is otherwise unrestricted*, but it develops fully if sexual restriction is general. Consequently, what is decisive for the child's health is *not the incest wish itself but the conditions under which it is experienced and dealt with*. Roheim continues:

Deparintja, otherwise a jolly fellow, is obviously depressed one day. We are in Hermannsburg and the descendants of the altjiranga matina (totemistic ancestors) go to the missionary school. 'Why are you so sad?' I ask him. After some hesitation he makes up his mind to tell me the reason. I already know it in advance. *He has been beaten by the missionary for having kissed a four-year-old girl. The missionary has given him a sound thrashing.* After a short pause he starts playing, asserting that the snake is sad. Then he makes the snake smell the vagina of the goat. Thereupon the snake is to marry the goat.[50] [Reich's italics]

If the scientific investigator Roheim did not regard the brutal beating of a child for a kiss given to a playmate as entirely in keeping with the 'natural order of things' and in the interest of the 'necessary discipline and order', he could not pass by such a phenomenon without asking himself why it is that the boy wants to marry the goat at this moment. Is that not a transference to an animal produced and fixed by the external denial of a natural interest? But again Roheim comes in with his depth psychology:

What Deparintja makes the snake do is his own crime ... he had kissed the girl's genital. For this he had been beaten. Now the game goes on and all the toy animals and dolls must smell the vagina and the anus of the monkey who has always been made to represent the mother of all these beings. Thereupon he has a big rubber doll perform as the chief and this chief thrashes all the other dolls and animals for having smelt the goat. In this connection it must be mentioned that in Hermannsburg the inkata is the head of the missionary station ... One of the many ways of expression in which the Oedipus complex manifests itself in the games ...

Something else is of interest: the very thing that Roheim so avidly bypasses confirms my viewpoint. Does not the game described by Roheim indicate an actual transformation in the beaten boy? Is that not the beginning of identification of the boy with God's apostle, an identification that has far-reaching consequences for the mass psychological development of the whole tribe? Does not the boy simply adopt as his own some-

50. [1951] See also the account of missionary influence on the sex-economy of primitives in *Top of the World*, by Hans Ruesch (Harper, 1950), which developed into red fascism, the most cruel suppression of life and love ever known to mankind.

thing that he had previously declined and that he will shortly apply to others? Is this not the phenomenon I described – the reproduction of a new social system in the character structure of the human beings subject to it; a small instance, it is true, but an exemplary one? Roheim writes in his 'criticism' of *Der Einbruch*:

Finally some examples may show that Reich draws conclusions from assumptions which do not answer to the facts. Reich writes, on page 22: 'But as moral sex education only enters into the history of mankind with the interest in private property and develops with it, neuroses are features of a society that has a patriarchal organization and private property.' When I attended the consecration of a Pitchentara boy I was told that he was treated indulgently, that he was not beaten too hard during the throwing up towards the sky because he was always a good boy, obeyed the old men and did not occupy himself too much with girls. The Pitchentara are certainly those humans on the earth whom one would be most justified in calling communist. By the way, they are organized neither matrilineally nor patrilineally, nor have they any promiscuity; jealousy is a main motive of their actions both in everyday life and in fairy tales – but it is to be hoped that not even Reich would maintain that here there exists class rule and capitalism.

No one has ever maintained that matriarchal primitives are communists, but rather that they have a *primeval* communist – i.e. work-democratic – form of society, which is not the same as the communism of the twentieth century. It is different from the patriarchal form both in economic and in sexual organization. There must be transition stages, too. On the basis of a comparison of the two fundamental social organizations, I distinguished two ways in which patriarchy evolves out of matriarchy: (1) an *internal* development through the mechanism of the marriage gift, the tribute from clan to clan, which Roheim himself describes without suspecting what it signifies; (2) a development arising out of *external* influences such as conquest by patriarchal tribes or the intrusion of white 'culture'. Within the matriarchal organization, then, the patriarchal beginnings must gradually emerge as special factors in the social environment. Thus, to begin with, only some of the children fall under the sway of asceticism; only some are subject to the pressure of pubertal sexual restriction; only some of the adults are subject to the coercion of permanent compulsory marriage. These embryonic forms of authoritarian patriarchy grow at the expense of matriarchal characteristics. I also believe that I was able to identify the point where mother-right becomes father-right. That occurs when the inheritance passes from the nephew of the mother's brother to his son. This is clear from Malinowski's material. However, Roheim states that there are people who are organized neither matriarchally nor patriarchally. If he had analysed his data from that point of view, he would not have maintained such impossibilities. All peoples show one of the two forms, or else they are in a transition stage; there is no third form.

The degree of openness with which (the children) Deparintja, Myiki, Iliakurla and the others talk about coitus and sexual perversions, as well as the exclusiveness and the clearness of the sexual meaning of their games, distinguish these children from those of our race.

It is an established fact that the children observed by Roheim behave exactly like those observed by Malinowski; the reports of their games are further proof of this. And, as though Roheim had fully accepted my ethnological theory, which is diametrically opposed to his, he concludes his report:

We have studied two groups of children both belonging to the same race: the missionary children go to school and their character has undergone a change in many respects although they have retained many features of the real children of the wilderness. The children of the bush, however, romp about, fight and have coitus with each other but I have never seen anything in them similar to the sadistic and masochistic playing in which Deparintja indulged (Deparintja is the boy who was beaten by the missionary). As we know, he has so often been punished for unhampered outbreaks of his natural instincts that indulgence in these impulses has come to be connected in his mind with the idea of tormenting or being tormented. The native originally has an aggressive character, it is true, but not a sadistic one. He may shout at a child in a fit of anger, he may even throw his boomerang at it, but he will hardly punish it deliberately. Thus the child of the bush never has the opportunity to acquire a sadistic super-ego through introjection and it will never learn to enjoy playing at punishing and being punished.

I could scarcely have wished for a better confirmation of the sex-economic concept. What can we deduce from the above?

That sadism is a *social* product resulting from the suppression of the natural infantile impulses of love, from the muscular diversion of libidinous energy;

that the explanation of this phenomenon must be looked for and will be found in the social intrusion of compulsory moral regulation of sex life;

that neuroses result from the patriarchal change of the social order and that capitalism is *not* a consequence of neuroses as Roheim thinks;

that sex life regulates itself spontaneously, sex-economically, according to natural laws, if it is not hindered;

that with the invasion of compulsory moral regulation, its permanent ideological motive, the necessity to control the instincts, is established in the form of unnatural, *secondary*, *anti-social* drives such as sadism and masochism; this applies to all perverse impulses. Human brutality is like an explosion, like a break from the prison in which human love life is held captive.

The confusion in Roheim's views has its parallel, though less grotesquely, in psychoanalysis wherever the scientific findings of psychoanalysis come into conflict with the psychoanalyst's moralistic outlook on life. A clear instance of this confusion is that he postulates and demonstrates the absence of sadism; yet, when describing a patriarchal tribe, the Aranda, he reports: 'In this social order a man can always obtain other young women either by brute force or by his authority as chief . . . The sadistic component of male sexuality can therefore be abreacted very well. Men and women have a natural cruelty.'

Thus, all's well with the world, and with us too. Sadism is a natural component of male sex life, and the Hungarian boyar can go on beating his wife, exactly as the Arandas do, for Roheim has 'shown how happy and untroubled the sexual life of the Aranda is; the husband, every inch a man, is his wife's lord and father.' That is not politics and not philosophy but 'objective research'! This is the opinion of the whole life-negating view of human affairs. But it can no longer claim to be objective and attempt to disavow our work with the reproach that we are politically biased.

WHAT MAKES ROHEIM IMPORTANT?

In a scientific controversy it is difficult fully to separate the subject matter from its advocate. As we have seen, a scientific concept does not hang suspended in mid-air but is inseparable from the structure, the thinking, and the social attitude of the scientist concerned. I think it right to emphasize at every opportunity that what is important is not whether research on human nature derives from a particular outlook on life and is coloured by it; that this cannot be otherwise is clear to any man of science. What is decisive is *what* outlook on life allies itself with a scientific activity. One outlook places the knowledge, the whole personality of the scientist, often his very existence, in the service of the investigation of life. The other proceeds in everything, literally everything – from the harmless erroneous formulation of theories to the boycotting and scientific plundering of the adversary to reactionary actions and pamphlets – with the aim, on the one hand, of securing the nimbus of scientific research for itself and, on the other hand, of concealing every item of knowledge laboriously acquired, of blunting it and side-stepping its consequences. Roheim is a shining example of this type of scientific attitude, and it is *for this reason* that he is important.

From this discussion, one can clearly see what the future tasks of sex-economy are. Let us summarize them:

The preservation and continuation of the psychosociological method of research is currently one of the most important tasks of every cultural and political investigator. We are confronted with the job of solving, once and for all, theoretically and practically, the problem that has dominated man subconsciously and consciously for thousands of years: *Can there be a social order fulfilling its function, the regulation of human relations and the safe-guarding of the gratification of the instinctual needs, without sexual suppression, sexual repression, and armouring?*

All hitherto existing cultural research asserts that there cannot be social order with freedom of the instincts. In opposition, sex-economy maintains and proves not only that such a social order exists and that it can exist but, in addition, that through the sex-economic regulation of love life, which presupposes full sex-affirmation instead of sex-negation, some of the great problems oppressing men's lives today can be solved for the first time, and that social democracy and real mass culture cannot begin until the love life of the working population of the earth is regulated sex-economically. As existing conflicts clamour for a solution, and as they will always eventually find one, the conflict between sexuality and morality, nature and culture, sexual life and work achievement, the individual and the collective, cannot, on principle, constitute the exception.

Here is the place to consider the following problems:

1. The sexual suppression dominating the masses, which finds its expression in superstition, mysticism of all kinds, inhibition of thinking, fear of authority, blind obedience, readiness to make sacrifices for the oppressors, etc., is the most powerful weapon of social tyranny. The sexual awakening of the masses, which also gives rise to their awareness of their economic plight, spells the end of tyranny.

2. Social sexual suppression creates the illnesses constituting mass plague. The elimination of sexual suppression is the most important prerequisite of a mass prophylaxis of emotional diseases.

3. Sexual inhibitions and disturbances ruin human intelligence, courage, sense of reality, and working capacity. The gap between the working capacity of man and his actual achievements and work interests is gigantic. A solution to the problem of the lack of a rational, joyful, co-operative work

process is impossible without social sex-economy. If this is erroneous, character-analysis and the orgasm theory are completely wrong.

4. The continued existence of any kind of religion and mysticism depends on the continued existence of sexual suppression and armouring of the bio-system. As long as the sex-economic regulation of sex life has not been established, a large-scale solution to these problems cannot be expected.

5. Every social system is reproduced ideologically in the character structure of its members, and structure formation is essentially a matter of sexual structure. In Soviet Russia, where the trend towards the alteration of the sexual structure made a clear breakthrough in the years 1918 to 1923, though the leaders of the revolution were not conscious of it, there is today [1931], to an ever-increasing extent, a contradiction between the economic foundation of socialism and human structure formation, resulting in the regression of an incipient socialist culture.[51] Essentially, the adaptation of man to the socialist economic system must be considered a failure there. But as every social system either reproduces itself in man libidinously or else endangers itself and, since man only, not dead productive power, is the driving force of social processes (which Marx knew when he based his theory on the difference between living and dead productive power), the problem of sex-economy is of vital importance to the Soviet Union.

These problems, which await study, justify our resolution to be unrelentingly, ruthlessly critical and to devote ourselves to serious, uncompromising work. Our path is laborious and socially dangerous, and reaching the target is therefore highly uncertain; the opposition of the authoritative and responsible leaders of present-day political parties, as well as of scientific circles, is enormous.

Our knowledge of human longing, of human structure and its contradictions, of the obstacles, both internal and external, standing in the way of the realization of a work-democratic, rational organization of society enables us, better than would mere instinctive resolution, to fight our way step by step.

51. *The Sexual Revolution.*

What today sounds incredible will some day be taken for granted. We are 'swimming against the current' but, in doing so, we have venerable predecessors. That we err here and there is certain. But it is just as certain that we are on the verge of disclosing the secrets of a cultural barbarism of thousands of years' duration and, in fact, that we are standing on the threshold of the sexual revolution of the future.

Index

MORE ABOUT PENGUINS
AND PELICANS

Penguinews, which appears every month, contains details of all the new books issued by Penguins as they are published. From time to time it is supplemented by *Penguins in Print*, which is a complete list of all titles available. (There are some five thousand of these.)

A specimen copy of *Penguinews* will be sent to you free on request. For a year's issues (including the complete lists) please send 50p if you live in the British Isles, or 75p if you live elsewhere. Just write to Dept EP, Penguin Books Ltd, Harmondsworth, Middlesex, enclosing a cheque or postal order, and your name will be added to the mailing list.

In the U.S.A.: For a complete list of books available from Penguin in the United States write to Dept CS, Penguin Books Inc., 7110 Ambassador Road, Baltimore, Maryland 21207.

In Canada: For a complete list of books available from Penguin in Canada write to Penguin Books Canada Ltd, 41 Steelcase Road West, Markham, Ontario.